STEPPING WESTWARD

The Inaugural Lectures of Professor Nigel Leask,
Regius Chair of English Language and Literature,
and Professor Alan Riach, Chair of Scottish Literature,
the University of Glasgow

Given on
2nd December 2006

Association for Scottish Literary Studies

First published in Great Britain, 2008
by the Association for Scottish Literary Studies
Department of Scottish Literature
7 University Gardens
University of Glasgow
Glasgow G12 8QH

in co-operation with
the University of Glasgow

British Library Cataloguing in Publication Data
A CIP record for this book is available from the
British Library

ISBN 978-0-948877-84-1

The Association for Scottish Literary Studies acknowledges
the support of the Scottish Arts Council towards the
publication of this book.

Scottish
Arts Council

Typeset by Ellipsis Books Ltd, Glasgow
Printed by Bell and Bain Ltd, Glasgow

Contents

'Stepping Westward'

We have adopted the title of Wordsworth's great poem of 1803 for this publication because it connects and articulates both the English and Scottish literary traditions, underlining the differences between them as well as the common ground which they share, a concern addressed by both our lectures.

Wordsworth's poem was written during a visit to the rainy Trossachs during his tour of Scotland in Autumn 1803; 'While my fellow travellers and I were walking by the side of Loch Ketterine, one fine evening after sunset, in our road to a Hut where, in the course of our Tour, we had been hospitably entertained some weeks before, we met, in one of the loneliest parts of that solitary region, two well-dressed Women, one of whom said to us, by way of greeting, "What, you are stepping westward?"'

> *"What, you are stepping westward?"*—*"Yea."*
> —'Twould be a wildish destiny,
> If we, who thus together roam
> In a strange Land, and far from home,
> Were in this place the guests of Chance:
> Yet who would stop, or fear to advance,
> Though home or shelter he had none,
> With such a sky to lead him on?

The dewy ground was dark and cold;
Behind, all gloomy to behold;
And stepping westward seemed to be
A kind of heavenly destiny:
I liked the greeting; 'twas a sound
Of something without place or bound;
And seemed to give me spiritual right
To travel through that region bright.

The voice was soft, and she who spake
Was walking by her native lake:
The salutation had to me
The very sound of courtesy:
Its power was felt; and while my eye
Was fixed upon the glowing Sky,
The echo of the voice enwrought
A human sweetness with the thought
Of travelling through the world that lay
Before me in my endless way.

But if the specific reference is to an English poet in Scotland, the metaphors of courtesy, curiosity, the securities of native dwelling and the loneliness of wandering in the human story have universal resonance. It's worth noting the way in which Iain Crichton Smith gently acknowledges the touch of this (as well as Wordsworth's beautiful companion poem 'The Solitary Reaper') in his poem, 'Two Girls Singing' from 1965, where, evoking his own loneliness on a night-time city bus, he suddenly recognises a human affinity, a kinship, in the voices he hears:

It neither was the words nor yet the tune.
Any tune would have done and any words.
Any listener or no listener at all.

As nightingales in rocks or a child crooning
in its own world of strange awakening
or larks for no reason but themselves.

So on the bus through late November running
by yellow lights tormented, darkness falling,
the two girls sang for miles and miles together

and it wasn't the words or the tune. It was the singing.
It was the human sweetness in that yellow,
the unpredicted voices of our kind.

It is the paradigm of our lectures that the visible connections and
reciprocal strengths of reading both Wordsworth and Crichton Smith
together depend upon a full understanding of the different national
cultural histories from which each of their voices emerge, these
different – and unpredicted – 'voices of our kind.'

Nigel Leask
Alan Riach

Introduction

It is a real pleasure to me briefly to introduce the two fine inaugural lectures of Professor Nigel Leask, Regius Professor of English Literature, and Professor Alan Riach, Chair of Scottish Literature, of the University of Glasgow. Both are friends and colleagues; more importantly, both are enthusiasts for their subject whose perspectives on English and Scottish literature – and literature generally – are refreshingly open, challenging categories and attitudes which to my mind need to be reviewed radically, both in terms of English and Scottish literatures' placing of themselves within the international context, and in terms of each other's recognition of the validity of their respective disciplines – and their constant interconnections.

What struck me as so positive and mutually enriching about the two lectures which were delivered in the new and impressive Charles Wilson Lecture Theatre in December 2006 is the way that they complemented each other. It was liberating and new to hear boundaries being crossed, with an underlying constant in both of mutual respect for the culture and tradition of others, whether these others be individuals, or constituents of region and nation, or even members of the academic structures which in Glasgow allow the several different but symbiotic approaches to literatures and languages. Both speakers were comfortable in setting their talks in a world context, Leask citing Amitav Ghosh, Conrad, and Homi Bhaba (to name a few) alongside John Home's *Douglas* and his central figure of Burns. Leask's Burns, however, is re-contextualised in ways which break down the all too shadowy lines between traditional romantic criticism, and the recent rise in Scottish critical reassessment of what it sees as traditions and creations in Scotland which can require revaluation in terms other than those applied for long in the study of 'English' literature. Here Burns is seen not as unfortunate outsider to the major romantics, but re-read in the light of his contemporaries as one of the major influences in developing romanticism – and stimulating Wordsworth and Coleridge in their quest for 'the real language of men'. With similar relocation of Byron, argued Professor Leask, 'both Burnsian and Byronic "mobility" here challenge Union, the organic stability of Anglo-British identity'. Even more subtle thereafter is Leask's seamless merging of his borderline revaluations with the work of his distinguished predecessor, the first holder of the Regius Chair in Glasgow, John Nicholl – with a fascinating and refreshing discussion of Nicholl's ground-breaking review of Burns's poetry and the man – rather than the man and his poetry.

These two inaugural lectures became mutually reinforcing. Professor Riach, enabled by his fourteen years in New Zealand to look at Scottish and British culture from across the world, developed perspectives allowing juxtapositions which surprised, then validated their inclusion – from West Indian novelist Wilson Harris to Donald Allen's ground-breaking *The New American Poetry* of 1960, or from the spaghetti western *Once Upon a Time in the West* which gave Riach his title and theme on confrontation of cultures in his part of Scotland. Professor Riach talked 'from the depths of my vulnerability' (and as a major Scottish poet) – and true to this, made a powerful and impassioned plea for not just Glasgow, but every Scottish university to have a Chair of Scottish Literature, asserting the validity of the subject in terms of the significantly different traditions and themes of that literature – but clearly, from the wide ranging international context of his talk, in no narrow and inward-looking way.

I am heartened and optimistic regarding the spirit in which Nigel Leask focussed on the debatable lands of Anglo-Scottish literature, and in which Alan Riach connected Scottish literature to the world. I am perhaps even more heartened by their obvious passion for the defence of literature. In a world of ever-recurring quality assurance exercises and research assessments, it is clear that for these two scholars and teachers, literature and its free academic and pedagogic consideration stands at the head of any other considerations. Stale boundaries begin to open, yet paradoxically fused with new respect for the validity and worth of the varieties of creative production in English and Scottish – and many other – literatures. I believe that the School of English and Scottish Language and Literature at Glasgow is unique in its tripartite approach to its subjects. In its recognition of cultural hyphenations in the relationships and border-crossings of English, Scottish, American and other literatures and languages, together with Scottish and Celtic studies generally, and its encouragement of creative writing, it will continue to stand at the forefront of liberal and liberating developments in Scotland, Britain – and beyond.

Douglas Gifford

'Across the Shadow Line': Robert Burns, Scottish Romanticism and the English Canon

Nigel Leask, Regius Chair of English Language and Literature

Inaugural Lecture delivered on 2nd December 2006 in the Sir Charles Wilson Theatre, Glasgow University

In September of this year I had the pleasure, like several others present today, of attending a big three-day conference at the University of Berkeley, California. Organised by Ian Duncan and Murray Pittock, it was entitled 'Scottish Romanticism in World Literatures'. To focus an international conference on Scottish writing of the period – especially envisaged within a global context – was a milestone in Romantic Studies, consolidating an important new direction in research and teaching.

I'll start with a brief travel narrative of my own experience of 'Stepping Westwards'. Waiting in line at Glasgow Airport for my American Airlines flight to San Francisco, via Chicago O'Hare, I was subjected to the tedious security checks inflicted on all air travellers in the aftermath of the latest terror panic. A uniformed Glaswegian security agent for American Airlines approached me while I waited and asked me a number of questions, including the purpose of my visit to the US. When she heard I was attending a conference on 'Scottish Romanticism' she pulled a wry face (she was a woman in her later twenties) and demanded, without the slightest hesitation: 'Does it exist'? Subjected to the same set of questions by another, older woman further down the line, the reaction was somewhat more positive: 'Och my man's really romantic, you know' – so Scottish romanticism was vindicated, to some extent at least. A weary ten hours later, going through US immigration in Chicago, the questioning ritual was repeated, this time by a tough-looking officer who was utterly stumped by my answer. 'Scottish romanticism? What is that?' Scott, Hogg, Baillie, Carlyle, etc. left him none the wiser, although he had heard of 'Bobbie' Burns, maybe because they shared a similar line of business. His puzzlement lifted when he heard that my destination (and the site of the apparently pointless conference) was San Francisco: 'We call it the city of fruits and nuts', he briskly informed me, leaving unsaid his obvious conviction that nuts, if not fruits, were precisely the sort of people who'd have opinions to share on the topic of 'Scottish Romanticism'.

When I mused on these airport exchanges (I promise you the quality of the discussion improved considerably once I got to Berkeley) it seemed appropriate that they were 'border questions', allowing for the fact that airports are where most of us here today cross borders. In my inaugural lecture I want to suggest that the question of Scottish romanticism was and is precisely a question of borders, a fact which has gained a new visibility for our generation. In a globalised era, national frontiers have become increasingly permeable to flows of capital, migration and information, as well (as we're constantly reminded) to Terror. In acknowledging the postmodern permeability of borders, I've borrowed the term 'shadow line', although I'm aware that this is a poor metaphor for the concrete walls constructed along the US/Mexican or Israeli/Palestinian frontiers, separating the haves from the have-nots in the global stakes.

The term itself comes from Amitav Ghosh's 1988 novel *The Shadow Lines,* an exploration of the often tragic human and political consequences of crossing colonial and post-colonial borders.[1] Ghosh's title in turn alludes to Joseph Conrad's late masterpiece *The Shadow-Line* (1916), a maritime *bildungsroman* set in the colonial far east, but whose title alludes to crossing a line 'from youth, carefree and fervent, to the more self-conscious and more poignant period of mature life.'[2] Both the outer and the inner, existential, boundaries between and within people are at stake in these novels, although the significance of the border experience has shifted from Conrad to Ghosh, with the break-up of the European colonial empires. Border crossing is also a concern of much recent work in postcolonial theory, from Homi Bhabha's essay 'Border Lives: The Art of the Present' to the work of Argentinian critic Walter Mignolo, whose 'border thinking' attempts to establish 'a geohistorical location that is constructed as a crossing instead of a grounding (e.g. the nation).'[3]

Rethinking the relationship between the local and the global around border crossings is of great importance in postcolonial literary studies. But does it give us any purchase on the cultural predicament of eighteenth and nineteenth-century Scotland? The heroine of John Home's 1756 historical tragedy *Douglas* laments the Anglo-Scottish conflict raging on either side of 'an ideal line / By fancy drawn', looking forward to a future era of Union.[4] The Scotland in which Home wrote was unusual in being bounded by a line which was at once an historic national border and a shadow line, in the sense of a post-union internal boundary. But if Scotland's shadow-line border once looked anomalous, not to say reprehensible, from the perspective of a twentieth century ethnic nationalism, it perhaps looks less so in an era of globalisation and mass emigration. Cultural identities are now less likely to be mapped by territorial filiation, or to be circumscribed by geopolitical borders, although in the light of recent developments on the edges of 'Fortress Britain' we should be sceptical about the rhetoric of easy, unobstructed trans-national flows of money, information and people. We live in a political climate when Scottish independence is once again on the political agenda, but the notion of a multi-cultural national community canvassed here looks refreshingly different from the earlier models of ethnic exclusivity. A new Scottish border might be open to Europe and the wider world, rather than miniaturising the defensive closure of the past. Seen through the optic of the present political moment, much of what appears to us as the confusion surrounding Scottish romanticism ('does it exist?') is a consequence of a border which was also a 'shadow line'. That's to say, despite its invisibility, a line which cast a long shadow upon the development of a supposedly 'homogenised' British, and imperial, culture.

Dr Johnson notoriously quipped 'the noblest prospect which a Scotchman ever sees, is the high road that leads him to England!'[5] Nevertheless, the published narrative of Dr Johnson's 1773 Highland *Tour*, and the management of the Scotophobic Doctor by an anxious James Boswell, were both defining moments in Anglo-Scots cultural relations. Boswell had attended Adam Smith's lectures on Rhetoric and Belles-Lettres while a student at Glasgow University in 1759–60, lectures which shaped many of his subsequent projects, including his great *Life of Johnson*.[6] One of my favourite moments in the *Edinburgh Journals*, illustrating Boswell's symptomatic identity complex, occurs when he complains of his wife Margaret's indifference to the 'turn for low life' in Fielding's novels. This, he wrote; went to show that 'she has nothing of that English *juiciness* of mind of which I have a great deal, which makes me delight in humour. But what hurts me more, she has nothing of that warmth of imagination which produces the pleasures of vanity and many others'.[7] It might be said in her defence that Margaret Boswell didn't need to read about low life, given that it was regularly wafted into her bedroom in the small hours of the morning.

As a Scot professing romantic literature, the question of 'Scottish romanticism' is obviously a matter of great personal as well as professional interest to me. All the more so given my privilege in occupying Glasgow's Chair of *English* Language and Literature. Since moving from the English Faculty at Cambridge in 2004 I've often wondered about the difference it makes teaching English literature in Glasgow to predominantly, although by no means exclusively, Scottish students. After all, a reconfigured and post-colonial relationship between the local and the global has decentred English studies wherever the subject is taught. Given that Glasgow University (uniquely) boasts a dedicated department of Scottish literature, what sort of disciplinary shadow line pertains between English and Scottish literature? Alan will have more to say about this later this afternoon, but the study of a distinct Scottish canon and the deep cultural contexts from which it emerges is also a consequence of the reconfiguration of the English canon which I'm investigating today.

When John Nichol was appointed to the first Regius Chair of English Language and Literature at Glasgow in 1862, he announced in his inaugural lecture that 'the map of language is the map of universal ethnology, and in the literature of a race, as in the strata of a land, we may read its history.'[8] Nichol was himself a Glaswegian, raised just up the hill in Dowanhill Observatory which his father occupied as Professor of Astronomy.[9] He had a particular interest in 'romantic' literature (though he still used the term in inverted commas), and published critical biographies of Burns, Byron and Carlyle. Although a committed Liberal and a supporter of Nationalist liberation in Hungary, Italy, Poland and most other places in the world (apart from Ireland and Scotland), Nichol wouldn't have recognised the existence of a distinct 'Scottish romanticism'.[10] Nor would his fellow Scot, Principal Shairp, Professor of Poetry at Oxford, who in 1879 published a study of Robert Burns in John Morley's 'English Men of Letters' series.[11] Shairp seemed oblivious to the anomaly, although there's much more at fault in his dreary, moralising study of Burns. Best of all though is Thomas Carlyle's priceless comment, in a letter to Goethe, that 'We English, especially we Scotch, love Burns.'[12]

The cultural affiliation of these Victorian Scots was 'English' because in linguistic terms they aspired to, or professed, *English* language and literature, a view underlined in the title of Nichol's Chair. Stefan Collini has observed that 'across a wide range of political and cultural activities, *English* nationalism has in fact been a vast presence in *British* history of the last two centuries (that is surely the right relation between the two adjectival forms), even although it has largely not been recognised as such or systematically articulated.'[13] There is, however, more to be said here, and I'll return to Nichol in the final section of my lecture, because the difficult question of nineteenth century Scottish identity is at once the legacy of 'Scottish romanticism,' and also the ideological matrix of the new Glasgow Regius Chair.

Is it perhaps the case that 'Scottish romanticism' is just a trendy neologism, a modish piece of academic repackaging hiding an intrinsic void or emptiness? New work on romanticism has begun to address the question in relation to the 'Four Nations' historiography of England, Scotland, Ireland and Wales, as in a recent collection of essays entitled *English Romanticism and the Celtic World*, edited by Gerry Carruthers and Alan Rawes.[14] In the introduction to another important recent contribution to this debate, *Scotland and the Borders of Romanticism,* the editors contrast a marginalised Scottish literary scene to the 'organic' English romantics Blake, Wordsworth, Coleridge and Keats. 'Scotland' they write, 'could only loom as an intermittent, shadowy, anachronism, a temporal as well as a spatial border of romanticism.'[15] Rather than being 'a site of romantic production, Scotland's fate is to have become a romantic object or commodity: glamorous scenery visited by the Wordsworths, Turner, Queen Victoria, steam-train parties of tourists; a series of kitsch, fake, more or less reactionary "inventions of tradition", from Ossian and Scott to Fiona MacLeod and *Brigadoon*.'[16] Not to mention the 'Tartan Monster': even the Lowlander Burns was by 1805 being represented the London print industry resplendent in a kilt.[17]

'Emptiness' is a word which resonates through accounts of Scottish literature of this period, from Dr Johnson's 'let us not fill the vacuity [of Gaelic literature] with *Ossian*' to (a couple of centuries later) Edwin Muir's description of the novels of Walter Scott as 'elaborate invention screening a curious emptiness.'[18] Muir's judgement was echoed by Tom Nairn in *The Break-Up of Britain* (1981), for whom Scott personified 'a larger emptiness', the lack of a 'a mature cultural romanticism' which in Nairn's analysis must be defined by an oppositional nationalist politics. Not that the 'black hole' in Scottish creative literature between 1831 and 1880 was a symptom of material stasis; on the contrary, Victorian Scotland saw huge social and industrial growth; emigration across the shadow line, to be sure, but also *immigration*, largely from Ireland, during which the population of Glasgow rose by 153%.[19]

Part of the problem seems to be the 'unromantic' legacy of the Scottish Enlightenment, the land of Cobbett's 'Scotch feelosophers',

"A Flight of Scotchmen", by R. Newton, 1794. Courtesy of the Lewis Walpole Library, Yale University. Thanks to Harriet Guest for drawing my attention to this print.

the *Edinburgh Review,* and the predatory relationship between (Byron's phrase) 'English Bards and Scotch Reviewers'. In a fiercely chauvinistic essay 'On the Scotch Character' William Hazlitt wrote that 'a Scotchman is a machine, and should be constructed on sound moral, and philosophical principles, or should be put a stop to altogether.'[20] One of the ironies of Hazlitt's essay (and Hazlitt is so slippery that it would be dangerous to designate him as a Scotophobe *tout court*) is that he insists upon projecting a strongly marked nationality upon those very nineteenth century Scots who were anxious to deny precisely that thing: 'The Scotch nation are a body-corporate. They hang together like a swarm of bees . . . A Scotchman gets on in the world because he is not one, but many . . . He is a double existence – he

Robert Burns, by
Alexander Nasmyth,
c.1821. Courtesy of the
National Portrait Gallery,
London.

stands for himself and his country.'[21] Yet Hazlitt was elsewhere forced
to make one important exception – for his praise of Walter Scott
was often qualified.

In his 1818 *Lectures on the English Poets* Hazlitt praised Robert Burns
as an incarnation of poetic genius, the antithesis of the abstract
'Spirit of the Age'; 'a real heart of flesh and blood beating in his
bosom'. Hazlitt's Burns belied all the stereotypical traits which he'd
foisted on the Scots; 'a man of genius is not a machine: . . .[poets]
live in a state of intellectual intoxication . . . it is too much to
expect them to be distinguished by peculiar *sang froid*, circum-
spection, and sobriety.'[22]

How then do we 'mind the gap' of Scottish romanticism? In what he has provocatively dubbed 'the Scottish invention of English literature' Robert Crawford argues that the 'growing wish for a 'pure' English in eighteenth century Scotland was not an anti-Scottish gesture, but [rather] a pro-British one.'[23] The parallel eighteenth-century Scottish invention in the field of creative writing was 'British Literature', although this was never as easily achieved as the Scottish Professoriate might have wished. 'I have often read & admired the Spectator, Adventurer, Rambler, & World' wrote Robert Burns in combative mood, 'but still with a certain regret that they were so thoroughly & entirely English. – Alas! Have I often said to myself, what are all the boasted advantages which my country reaps from a certain Union, that can counterbalance the annihilation of her Independence, & even her very name!'[24] Nevertheless, as Crawford has argued, Burns elsewhere proudly described himself as 'a Briton' and 'in his verse he deployed a *Lingua Britannica* which, in its constantly shifting mix, illustrates how a truly "British" language might have operated.'[25] In differentiating 'British' from 'English' Literature in its modern definition, Crawford argues that the Scottish example possesses enormous proleptic importance for contemporary anglophone post-colonial and world literatures encompassing 'the varieties of English'.[26]

In his 1996 study *Out of History*, Cairns Craig quarrels with the notion of Victorian Scotland as a cultural vacuum, proposing rather that it has been 'retrospectively evacuated by its historians.'[27] For some nationalists, such a gap legitimises the desire to create for Scotland 'a mirror-image of that claimed for English culture' out of despair at its peripheral, fragmented status.[28] As David Lloyd observes in the analogous case of Ireland, in his study of the brilliant, flawed romantic poet James Clarence Mangan; 'it is the failing of [nineteenth century]

Irish nationalism never to have questioned the idealism of identity thinking, which, even in its resistance to imperialism, links it closely to imperialist ideology.'[29]

In rejecting this idealism, we might instead ponder Cairns Craig's proposal that 'cultural analysis is the analysis of what happens *between* cultures, and in the ways in which cultural space is penetrated and shaped by the pressure of other cultural spaces'.[30] It's very much in the spirit of the Shadow Line that Susan Manning interprets the greatest work of Scottish philosophy, Hume's *Treatise of Human Nature*, as 'preserving a space where Union and the fragmenting, seceding impulse can co-exist in relations of association.'[31] In our current condition of post-modernity and post-coloniality, Scotland's 'drouthy' predicament (lamented by metropolitan snobs and self-hating nationalists alike) might actually be a *better* paradigm than the organic model supposedly represented by the English 'centre'; (Cairns Craig again) 'fragmentation, disunity, the lack of a continuous history, might represent more truly both the typical conditions of human culture and the foundations of originality than the "unities" and "maturities" that are part of the ideology of cultural domination.'[32]

Burns's Afterlives.

But this is by no means to go on the defensive. Take the case of Robert Burns, Scotland's greatest poet. Murray Pittock has recently drawn attention to the depressing fact of Burns's 'diminishing reputation in academic literary studies on both sides of the Atlantic' and noted the contrast between 'a confined realm of celebratory anaphora in Scotland and neglect abroad.'[33] Yet this was not always the case: from the beginning, and to an extent that hasn't been fully recognised, Burns exerted an immense influence on the development of romantic and nineteenth century English poetry and criticism.

Although English writers like Cowper, Coleridge, Wordsworth and Lamb enthused about Burns during his lifetime, the really significant event in the posthumous transmission of his poetry was the publication, in 1800, of Dr James Currie's *Works of Robert Burns*, prefaced by a 335-page critical biography of the poet which makes up the whole of the first of its four volumes. Currie, a Scottish 'Mad-doctor' residing in Liverpool (he was founder of the city's Insane Asylum), composed his memoirs of Burns 'not with the view of their being read by Scotchmen only, but also by natives of England, and of other countries where the English language is spoken or understood.'[34] It went through five editions and about 10,000 copies by 1805, reaching a 20th edition by 1820, and transmitted Burns to all the major writers of the romantic period.

A deep ambivalence lies at the heart of Currie's presentation of Burns, which has given him a bad reputation in Burns scholarship. On the one hand he sought to counter Henry Mackenzie's famous description of the Ayrshire Bard as a 'heaven-taught Ploughman', a sort of vulgar nine days' wonder. Although Burns was indeed 'a Scottish peasant', Currie argued, the Scottish peasantry 'possess a degree of intelligence not generally found among the same class of men in the other countries of Europe.' [Currie, I, 3]. Currie's Burns isn't really a romantic bard at all, but rather a vehicle for the promotion of Scottish enlightenment, industry and domestic virtue across the shadow line. Because Burns's poems, and particularly songs, had captured the patriotism and *gemeinschaft* which were such strong features of rural Scottish society, Currie viewed his poetry as embodying a sort of Scottish nationalism *under erasure*; 'it may be considered as a monument, not to his own name only, but to the expiring genius of an ancient and once independent nation' [Currie, I, 31].

The patriotism evoked here is an ingrained Scottishness of the mind, cemented by nostalgic association with childhood and the past, but at the same time one physically removed from any actual Scottish 'lifeworld'. Striding across the border to England and the colonies under the banner of Burns, Currie's Scottish peasantry *reculant pour mieux sauter*, look back the better to march forward, in the service of a British and imperial futurity.

Currie rightly sensed that the neglect of radical Burns around the time of his premature death in 1796 was a deep rebuke to the Scottish Tory establishment. So, '[Burns's] biographer' he argued, 'must keep [his vices] in mind, to prevent him from running into those bitter invectives against Scotland, &c., which the extraordinary attractions and melancholy fate of the poet naturally provoke.'[35] Drawing upon his medical training, Currie diagnosed the poet's vices as the result of uncontrolled passions and a pathological weakness of will of the sort frequently afflicting men of genius. 'In Dumfries,' Currie admonished, 'temptations to the sin that so easily beset him continually presented themselves; and his irregularities grew by degrees into habit . . . He who suffers from pollution of inebriation, how shall he escape other pollutions?' [Currie I, 205]. Although Currie's charges were later denied by Burns's brother Gilbert they elicited a spirited attack from William Wordsworth in his 1816 *Letter to a Friend of Robert Burns*, which included an invective upon Currie's intrusive, Boswellian biographical method.

Herein lies Currie's ambivalence in transmitting the Burns legacy, for the poet's 'besetting sin' became part of the posthumous legend.

William Wordsworth, by
Benjamin Haydon, 1842.
Courtesy of the National
Portrait Gallery, London.

Nearly all English responses to Burns in the romantic period are
reactions, in one way or another, to Currie's Burns. Most importantly,
they attempt to extract Burns from Scotland and Scottishness, denying
any causality between Scotland's enlightened peasantry and Burns'
genius. This latter point was, ironically, best expressed by Carlyle, the
stonemason's son from Ecclefechan: 'A Scottish peasant's life was the
meanest and rudest of all lives, till Burns became a poet in it, and a
poet of it . . . Is not every new genius an impossibility till he appear?'[36]
Despite the linguistic difficulties of Burns's 'poems chiefly written in
the Scottish dialect' for English readers, Burns was hailed as a founding
spirit of English romanticism. But like the young Bristol poet Thomas
Chatterton his genius was overcast by a tragic shadow.

Witness Wordsworth's famous lines in *Resolution and Independence,* hailing Burns as

> . . . Him who walked in glory and in joy
> Following his plough, along the mountain-side:
> By our own spirits are we deified:
> We Poets in our youth begin in gladness;
> But thereof come in the end despondency and madness.[37]

Burns's grave in Dumfries and birthplace cottage in Alloway rapidly became priority sites for English literary pilgrims, challenging the eighteenth century tourist monopoly of Shakespeare's

John Keats, by Joseph Severn, 1821–3. Courtesy of the National Portrait Gallery, London.

Stratford. Visiting the grave with her brother during their 1803 Scottish tour, Dorothy Wordsworth commented 'there is no thought surviving in connection with Burns's daily life that is not heart-depressing'.[38]

Knocking back the whisky toddies in Burns's birthplace cottage at Alloway in July 1818, by now a tavern benefiting from the poet's posthumous fame, John Keats penned a 'flat sonnet' and wrote to his friend Reynolds: 'One song of Burns's is of more worth to you than . . . a whole year in his native country. [Burns's] misery is a dead weight upon the nimbleness of one's quill – I tried to forget it – to drink Toddy without any Care – to write a merry Sonnet – it won't do – he talked with Bitches – he drank with Blackguards, he was miserable – We can see horribly clear in the works of such a man his whole life, as if we were God's spies.'[39] For Keats, Burns was a romantic genius despite (not because of, the gist of Currie's argument), what he called the poet's 'anti-grecian' Ayrshire environment. Later in the nineteenth century, for Matthew Arnold, the poet's genius itself had become tainted by a squalid parochialism, and one can see here how Currie's diagnostic reading of Burns's infirmities has become detached from the Scottish patriotism inflecting his biography: '[Burns's] world of Scotch drink, Scotch religion, and Scotch manners is against a poet, not for him, when it is not a partial countryman who reads him; for in itself it is not a beautiful world, and no one can deny that it is of advantage to a poet to deal with a beautiful world. Burns's world of Scotch drink, Scotch religion and Scotch manners is a harsh, a sordid, a repulsive world.'[40]

It is easy to miss, in all this invective, the degree to which Burns's poetry influenced the practice of English romantic poets, still, surprisingly, a hugely under-researched topic in romantic studies. Part of the problem, especially in the case of Wordsworth, maybe lies in the depth at which Burns's work was assimilated. Wordsworth generously acknowledged the extent of Burns's influence in his poem 'At the Grave of Burns', written in the Habbie stanza: 'whose light I hailed when first it shone, / And showed my youth / How verse may build a princely throne / On humble truth.'[41] Daniel Roberts has shown that Wordsworth and Coleridge were reading Currie's edition of Burns in September 1800, the very month in which they were composing the Preface to *Lyrical Ballads*, usually seen as the most important manifesto of the British romantic movement.[42] This explains why, whereas the Advertisement to the 1798 edition declares that the model for its poetic 'experiments' is 'the language of conversation in the middle and lower classes of society',[43] the 1800 Preface (composed after the poets had read Currie on Burns and the Scottish peasantry) specifies 'low and rustic life' as the social locus of 'the real language of men in a state of vivid sensation'.[44]

I think the rather abstract claims of Wordsworth's famous 'Preface to *Lyrical Ballads*' make more sense if we read Wordsworth's 'real language of men in a state of vivid sensation' as an excited response to Burns, and to Currie's account of Burns as an enlightened Scottish peasant. It's as if Wordsworth is de-territorialising Burns (and we should remember that Wordsworth is a border poet), removing him from his Scottish context, at the same time as appropriating the vernacular passion and radical energy of his poetry for English romanticism. I've argued elsewhere that in pursuing this goal, Wordsworth needed to devise an alternative language for poetry (impossibly) based on a rural lower-class vernacular that was not a regional dialect.[45] Poems like 'Michael' and 'The Brothers' published in the 1800 volume explicitly deny Currie's exceptionalist claims for the virtues of the Scottish peasantry, while drawing heavily on Burnsian models like 'The Cotter's Saturday Night.' But much more work still requires to be done on this subject.

Lord Byron, by
Thomas Phillips, c. 1835.
Courtesy of the National
Portrait Gallery, London.

Time permits only one final instance of Burns's deep influence, in relation to Lord Byron. Despite Carlyle's comparison of the two poets in his 1828 essay, it was the Irish poet Thomas Moore who first dwelt on Burns's poetic importance for Byron in his authorised 1830 biography of the latter poet. Although a fashionable figure in Regency London society, Moore was a life-long antagonist of the 1800 Union with Ireland, and much of his poetry was a more or less concealed lament for a lost Irish *patria*. In an 1807 letter Moore described his best-selling *Irish Melodies* as an expression of the instability of Irish feeling, 'that rapid fluctuation of spirits, that unaccountable mixture of gloom and levity'. 'If Burns had been an Irishman (and I would willingly give up all our claims to Ossian for him)', he added, 'his heart would have been proud of such music'.[46] Moore deftly handles his own indebtedness to Burns's songs by joining up the Celtic peripheries and appropriating him as an honorary Irishman.

Moore described how 'wee Geordie' Byron's romantic love of landscape was fed by the 'dark summit of Lachin-y-gair' during the period when he resided in Aberdeen with his Scottish mother, Catherine Gordon of Gight. He quoted Byron's lines from *Don Juan:* 'but I am half a Scot by birth, and bred / A whole one; and my heart flies to my head /As "Auld Lang Syne" brings Scotland, one and all—'.[47] Yet Byron resisted the temptation to pursue a career in Bardic Nationalism, attempting in his own words to '"scotch" the Scotchman in his blood'. This was partly a result of his tempestuous relationship with his Scottish ma, but also indicates his preference for a cosmopolitan identity. 'Half of those Scotch and Lake troubadours' he wrote, 'are spoilt by living in little circles and petty societies.'[48] Given this judgement, it's perhaps surprising to discover the aristocratic Byron's passionate and personal identification with the plebeian Burns, whose poetry he read in Currie's edition. Moore made much of Byron's reaction to reading some of Burns's *Merry Muses* in manuscript (songs that certainly didn't make it into Currie): 'What an antithetical mind! – tenderness, roughness – delicacy, coarseness – sentiment, sensuality – soaring and grovelling, dirt and deity – all mixed up in one compound of inspired clay!'[49]

Richard Cronin has noted that 'the impossibility of adequate biography' is 'an unlikely but common theme [amongst Byron's many biographers], a consequence of the extreme "mobility" that [they] all . . . recognise in him'.[50] But Byron's own description of 'antithetical' Burns I think offers a clue to Moore's own attempt to pin down his subject. Because the delicate matter of Byron's own divorce is such a central episode in his biography, the story of his parents' failed marriage is often overlooked. For Moore, however, Lord Byron, despite his noble pedigree, was the product of a spectacular failure of Anglo-Scottish Union, the disastrous marriage of Catherine Gordon and English 'Mad Jack' Byron. In fact Byron's whole identity *resists* union: 'So various indeed, and contradictory, were [Byron's] attributes, both moral and intellectual', Moore continued, 'that he may be pronounced not one, but many'.[51] Gesturing towards Byron's Scottishness on his maternal side, Moore here travesties Hazlitt's chauvinistic judgement; 'A Scotchman gets on in the world, because he is not one, but many.'[52] Rather than being a body corporate, as in Hazlitt's caricature of Scottishness, and in direct defiance of Currie's view of Burns, both Burnsian and Byronic 'mobility' here challenge Union, the organic stability of Anglo-British identity.

John Nichol's Burns and English Studies at Glasgow.

Relieved to discover that an earlier Glasgow Regius had published a book on Burns, I turned to John Nichol's 1882 study of the poet (*Robert Burns: A Summary of his Career and Genius*)[53] which led me on to his other publications. I hadn't any great expectations, mindful of George Davie's judgement in *The Democratic Intellect* that '[Nichol] the Glasgow Oxonian and friend of Swinburne [saw the] peculiar importance of English studies as a means of civilising the uncouth Scots'.[54] I quickly found out how wrong Davie was, and how far my admiration for Nichol exceeded initial expectations. The man who turned to Liberal Unionism in 1884 would hardly have recognised 'Scottish romanticism' as a legitimate description. But unlike his eighteenth century predecessor at Glasgow, Adam Smith (both men were Snell Exhibitioners from Glasgow to Balliol College, Oxford), Nichol

John Nichol and 'The Old Mortality Club', Balliol College, Oxford.

Professor
John Nichol.

certainly did have a distinct notion of the importance of Scottish writing in the development of the English literary canon.

In his inaugural lecture of 1862, Nichol distinguished the new Glasgow Chair of English from the older Scottish Rhetoric and Belles-Lettres Chairs, as well as the Oxford Chair of Poetry, recently occupied by Matthew Arnold. Its scope was 'at once narrower and wider . . . narrower as it is definitely restricted to one language [i.e. English] – wider because [it] is intended to be philological and historical, as well as critical, in its aims.'[55] The nationalism underpinning the rise of English studies (upon which I commented above) is evident in Nichol's belief that English was 'the most complete [language] in Europe . . . because it has enriched itself by receiving so many contributions'[56] from Celtic, Scandinavian, Saxon, Latin and Norman French. (It's interesting to compare this with Matthew Arnold's *Study of Celtic Literature,* published just four years later.) Nevertheless, '*Shakespeare and Burns*' wrote Nichol, 'are at this day read from the banks of the Connecticut and the Columbia river to the sands of Sydney and the Yellow Sea. At the close of the century, it is calculated that English will be spoken by at least 150 millions of human beings'[57] (my italics). Not only is Burns named alongside Shakespeare here, but Nichol's notion of English incorporates the anglophone USA as well as the British Empire. In one of the few recent studies of Nichol as a critic, Andrew Hook has underlined his importance in pioneering the academic study of American literature, a tradition appropriately continued today in Glasgow's Andrew Hook Centre for American Studies.[58]

Nichol's book on Burns stands out like a shining light from the murky stream of Victorian Burns biography. Anticipating the methods of modern criticism, 'Nichol used the life to illuminate the work, rather than the other way round,' as Philip Hobsbaum has noted.[59]

Aligning himself with Matthew Arnold's defence of culture as getting to know 'the best that has been thought and said' against the philistines and barbarians of Victorian Britain, Nichol was nevertheless irritated by Arnold's Scotophobia in his remarks on Burns, what he called his 'damned iteration' of 'Scotch drink, Scotch religion, and Scotch manners.' Burns's 'excess of patriotism' in songs such as 'Such a Parcel of Rogues' opened him to charges of provincialism, he conceded, in the eyes of the metropolitan critics like Arnold.[60] But Nichol also insisted that Burns was legitimately 'a national rather than a peasant poet', earning that title both for his gift of satirising Scottish vices, as for his power of 'elevating and intensifying our northern imagination.'[61] This was refreshing in an era when, as Richard Finlay remarks, the 'Scottish middle class were remarkably successful in their

An older
John Nichol.

ability to 'see ithers as oursels' [rather than vice versa] and in doing so turned Burns into a paradigm of Scottish bourgeois virtue.'[62]

Nichol the religious sceptic certainly can't be accused of letting Holy Willie off the hook, and he also showed sympathy with Burns's revolutionary politics: 'Over the house of Brunswick it has never been found possible to be poetically enthusiastic,'[63] he proclaimed with his usual dry humour. Quoting Currie's remark that Burns was a 'monument to the expiring genius of an ancient and independent nation', Nichol added that if he was 'the last of the old', he was also the 'first of the new' as poet of a democratic Britain.[64] He abstained from moralising on Burns's 'besetting sin' of alcoholism, but was happy to admit that the poet was indeed 'passion's slave'; 'more reckless in his loves than Lord Byron, almost as much so as King David.'[65] Of the bawdy *Merry Muses of Caledonia*, 'some were amusing, others only rough' but like Chaucer, Burns owed half his power to 'the touch of Bohemianism that demands now and then a taste of wild life.'[66] Nichol evidently felt that Victorian Scotland needed more, not less, of that 'Bohemian spirit'.

Reflecting on Burns's role in the development of Scottish literature, it's interesting that Nichol nominated the Paisley weaver-poet Robert Tannahill as his poetic successor, without even mentioning James Hogg, 'The Ettrick Shepherd.' And great as Scott and Carlyle were as prose writers, neither had approached Burns's genius for combining power and passion with musical expression. 'In this respect', Nichol continued in a highly significant critical judgement, 'his only heir was the future Lord of English verse, the boy who was about to leave the shadows of Loch-na-gair for the groves of Newstead.'[67] We're back here with Byron. But unlike Thomas Carlyle, who compared the two poets in order to belittle Byron, Nichol saw a more positive connection. 'Burns', he wrote, 'is the ancestor of

Wordsworth, to whom he bequeathed his pathetic interpretation of nature; and of Byron, the inheritor of his "passions wild and strong".'[68]

Nichol here picked up on earlier judgements in his 1880 study of *Lord Byron* for Morley's *English Men of Letters* series. In the earlier book he weighed into the conventional wisdom that sundered Byron from the Scottish literary tradition.[69] This resulted from a false stereotyping of the 'canny Scot' which, Nichol complained, 'is apt to make the critics forget the hot heart that has marked the early annals of the country, from the Hebrides to the Borders, with so much violence, and at the same time has been the source of so much strong passion and persistent purpose.'[70] Like Tom Moore, Nichol picked up on Byron's self-description in his account of Burns's 'antithetical mind . . . dirt and deity – all mixed up in one compound of inspired clay.'[71] But he didn't, of course, go so far, Regius Professor as he was, to read Byron's decentred cosmopolitanism as a challenge to the English canon, or organic integrity of the British Empire.

The influence of Nichol's judgements here seems to go in two directions. One, the unionist direction, shaped Lord Rosebery's remark in his 1896 speech to a Glasgow audience on the occasion of Burns's centenary that 'the two great natural forces in British literature' are Shakespeare and Burns (the audience apparently applauded his use of 'British' here.)[72] The other, more unexpected, issued in Hugh MacDiarmid's later essay 'The Neglect of Byron' (collected in *The Raucle Tongue),* that 'Byron was beyond all else a Scottish poet – the most nationally typical of Scottish poets, not excluding Burns. He answers – not to stock conceptions, the grotesque Anglo-Scottish Kailyard travesty, of Scottish psychology – but to all the realities of our dark, difficult, unequal and inconsistent national temper.'[73] The nationalist MacDiarmid clearly risks simply replacing the usual anodyne stereotype of Scottish character with a darker version of the same.

But despite his difficulties in wresting Burns from the sterile cult which surrounded him in twentieth century Scotland, in MacDiarmid's judgement the submerged notion of a fragmented, antithetical, decentred Scottish romanticism 'across the shadow line' is beginning to come up for air.

I think we still can learn from Nichol in a post-devolutionary Scotland where concerns about cultural identity in a globalised world are less strongly shaped by ideologies of Union and Empire. Nichol saw the study of English literature as a means of cultivating imagination, crossing the shadow line in order to combat provincialism and narrowness of thought, and this is still a worthy aspiration today. Ironic, then, that one of the reasons for the establishment of Glasgow's Regius Chair of English in 1862 was the introduction of competitive examinations for the Indian Civil Service, in which over a quarter of total possible marks were awarded for proficiency in English language and literature. Thomas Macaulay, the architect of the scheme, believed that training in English literature would endow 'men who represent the best part of our English nation' in the colonies; he looked forward to the propagation of 'that literature before the light of which impious and cruel superstitions are fast taking flight on the banks of the Ganges . . . And, wherever British literature spreads, may it be attended by British virtue and British freedom!'

Here we see 'Englishness' or (possibly in a concession to Macaulay's own Scottish roots) 'Britishness' being constructed in the mirror of the colonial other.[74] The British empire would be run by men who knew how (to cite some of the exam questions set in the mid 1850s) 'write out the plot of Shakespeare's "Lear", and mention the most remarkable characters of that play'; or else 'Mention the most important of Pope's literary friends, describe briefly their leading characteristics, and give a short account of one of the most celebrated works of each', etc. etc.[75] The Indian Civil Service report of 1855 presciently 'inclined to think that the examinations for situations in the Civil Service of the East India Company will produce an effect which will be felt in every seat of learning throughout the country.'[76]

Scottish university students, who had traditionally hoovered up many of the best jobs in the colonies, found themselves excluded from the glittering prizes because they weren't taught English literature. As W.G. Blackie complained at a Glasgow meeting of the Scottish Academical Institute in 1858, 'where is the provision made in Scotland for enabling our youth to equip themselves for so searching an examination?'[77] 'I cannot shut my eyes to what appears to me to be one of the most glaring defects of [Glasgow University]', he continued, 'the want of Professorships of the English Language, literature, and history.'[78] Although the ICS exam was clearly a case of the tail wagging the dog (rather like today's RAE or even AHRC), the University Commission of 1858 quickly established English as a university subject, and Queen Victoria endowed Glasgow's Chair in English with John Nichol as the first incumbent. This makes sense of the otherwise mysterious reference to the Indian Civil Service exams in Nichol's inaugural lecture.[79] Given my own interest in colonial and post-colonial literature, it seems both ironic, and appropriate, that my Chair originated as a means of facilitating the passage of Glasgow students across the colonial shadow line.

In a more positive light, Nichol initiated an approach to Scottish university education, and to his new discipline, which still flourishes today in a very different world. Advocating a combination of critical, historical and philological approaches to literature, Nichol believed that English should be closely linked to philosophy. He was also of the opinion that English Honours (as opposed to the ordinary classes) should include a paper on British history; given that there was no Chair of History in Glasgow until the 1890s, this meant that the Honours school in English wasn't launched until after he'd retired, under the auspices of the Shakespeare scholar A.C. Bradley, who was altogether less enthusiastic about the historical element.[80]

Although Nichol was himself a pretty dire poet and playwright, he did underline the importance of English composition and what we might call an 'ethics of style'; commanding the resources of our own language is still a vital concern for the teaching and learning of English literature, and I'm sure Nichol would have approved of Glasgow's Edwin Morgan Centre for Creative Writing. As sole English professor in the university, Nichol gave 160 lectures a year to two classes of 300 students each, but still somehow found time to pioneer extension lecturing across the UK from Dundee to Penzance; as his Victorian biographer wrote, 'there are hundreds who look back to his extra academical lectures . . . as their first initiation into the wide realm of English literary education'.[81] Nichol's initiative still flourishes in the university's Department of Adult and Continuing Education and the Arts Faculty's Continuing Professional Development provision, in the civic and anti-elitist spirit of his educational mission.

Although I'm aware that far too much of what I've said today has focussed on the boys, on male writers and a male canon, we shouldn't forget that from its inception the study of English literature was largely a female pursuit, much more so than cognate subjects like history, classics or philosophy. Once again Nichol deserves an honorary mention, although some of the credit should doubtless go to the inspiration of his step-mother Elizabeth Pease, a prominent Quaker abolitionist and feminist.[82] In the late 1860s

No. 6—Vol. III. GLASGOW, JANUARY 21, 1891. Price One Penny.

Studies of Students in Black and White.

No. IV.—TYPES FROM QUEEN MARGARET.

'Types from Queen Margaret's', *University of Glasgow Magazine*,
21 Jan 1891. Courtesy of the Glasgow University Archives.

he co-launched a series of academic 'Lectures for Ladies' which
he delivered in the Corporation Galleries in Sauchiehall Street. This
became 'the launching pad for a range of activities that led to the
regular admission of women to Glasgow University, via the foun-
dation of Queen Margaret College in 1877'.[83] English was extremely
popular with women students, and the QMC class of 1888 attracted
98 takers, as opposed to a meagre two for Latin.[84] As Chris Baldick
notes, such 'classes for women were not designed to emancipate,
but to confirm women in their established roles.'[85] Nevertheless,
there was certainly a submerged feminist potential in the study of
English literature, even more than its role as a springboard for

encouraging women to enter professional life, and one which would largely reshape our discipline in the later decades of the twentieth century.

Finally, and I promise that this is my closing shot, Nichol saw the study of literature as a means of countering the spirit of narrow specialisation and market-driven policy which was such a dominant feature of the Victorian era, and which is again, alas, resurgent in British universities. In a pamphlet bitterly attacking the University Reform Bill of 1888, Nichol cited Fichte's *Vocation of the Scholar* and complained that the traditional Scottish university curriculum with its generalist emphasis was being overtaken by 'the demands of a utilitarianism apt to set exclusive store on production and exchange, and to weigh too lightly the strengthening of our will, the refinement of our taste, and the enlarging of our sympathies.'[86] It's perhaps tempting to misread this as merely a bid to 'Hellenise' a philistine Scottish middle class, an elitist Oxonian legacy of Nichol's days at Balliol, as George Davie does (although, ironically, Nichol would have agreed with much in Davie's book). The target of Nichol's pamphlet was actually the Conservative government in London which had sanctioned a massive attack on the traditional culture of the Scottish universities, above all the generalist approach to higher education which he felt was best represented by the study of English, History and Philosophy.[87] The following year, in 1889, Nichol resigned his Chair after 27 years, exhausted and embittered.

While reluctant to criticise the gentlemanly ethic still prevailing at Oxford and Cambridge, Nichol was proud to emphasise that the Scottish universities were quite distinct insofar as they remained 'seminaries for the nation: *comparatively* poor, they are institutions for the *comparably* poor. Slenderly recruited from the upper class, but open in practice as well as theory to the more thrifty, intelligent or aspiring of the lower, they are in effect great public schools for the bulk of the middle class of the country.'[88] Although there's a touch of Victorian paternalism here in Nichol's talk of thrift and aspiration, I think that his pride in the social outreach of Scottish universities is something with which we can still identify, especially in a university which admits 86% of its students from the State sector.

It may be the case, as John Guillory has proposed, that the study of literature no longer endows the 'professional-managerial middle class' with desirable cultural capital.[89] Yet there's no sign of our undergraduate numbers declining, even with ever-increasing pressures on young people to knuckle down to gainful employment. If anything English literature continues to grow in popularity compared to many other academic subjects, and I'm moved by the number of our students who finance a non-vocational degree in English by working long shifts in Tescos or making other sacrifices. Nichol worried that Glasgow students worked too hard, smoked too much, and didn't take enough exercise.[90] He hoped they might 'chill out' a bit (not his own words of course), but I don't need to endorse that thought, given that our students hardly need instruction in this area, least of all from their teachers!

I think there's also an extraordinarily modern ring to Nichol's verdict on his own profession: 'of all the sins of which the present generation of University teachers can be accused the last is want of devotion to their duties, in the performance of which they have during the last two decades doubled their work[load] till, even by a keen adversary, it is admitted to have in some instance become "enormous".'[91] Exactly the same might be said in 2006 for my colleagues here in Glasgow, and in other universities around the country, and it is to these devoted colleagues, as well as our students, that my inaugural lecture is dedicated.

Thank you all for coming along to my inaugural lecture, and for your patience in listening to discussion of matters which are I hope 'academic' in the positive rather than negative sense so often heard today. It's wonderful to see so many of my friends, colleagues and students, and a special welcome to my aunt Alison Wolfe Murray and cousin Ronald Leask, and my sisters Deirdre and Josephine, all of whom have travelled far to be with me today, and to make up for the sad absence of our parents. Special thanks also to the Dean, Professor Elizabeth Moignard, and the Head of English Dr Nicky Trott for supporting these lectures and making the day financially possible, to my wife Evelyn for the PowerPoint images (and everything else!) and to Pat Devlin, Wendy Burt, and others who have helped with organisation. It's rather a scary thought that Nichol occupied the Regius Chair for 27 years, and that I'm only the seventh since: it's a daunting record of longevity which I'm already too old to match, you'll be glad to hear. But I'm personally happy to think that I've crossed back over to this side of the shadow line for good, I feel privileged to occupy the Glasgow Regius Chair, and I look forward to giving you my best in years to come. Thank you again.

Notes

1   Amitav Ghosh, *The Shadow Lines* (New Delhi: Ravi Dayal and Permanent Black, 1998).

2   Joseph Conrad, *The Shadow-Line* (Oxford: World Classics, 2002), p.111.

3   Homi K. Bhahba, Introduction to *The Location of Culture* (London and New York: Routledge, 1994), pp.1–18; Walter D. Mignolo, *Local Histories/Global Designs: Coloniality, Subaltern Knowledge, and Border Thinking* (Princeton UP, 2000), p.69.

4   Rev. John Home, *Douglas: A Tragedy. As it is acted at the Theatre-Royal at Covent Garden* (London, 1757), Act 1, sc.1, p.4.

5   James Boswell, *The Life of Johnson*, ed. R.W. Chapman, rev. ed. J.D. Fleeman, with introduction by Pat Rogers, World's Classics Edition (Oxford: Oxford University Press, 1980), p.302.

6   See Gordon Turnbull, 'James Boswell: Biography and the Union' in *The History of Scottish Literature, vol 2, 1660–1800*, ed. Andrew Hook, gen ed. Cairns Craig (Aberdeen: Aberdeen University Press, 1987), pp.157–174.

7   *Boswell's Edinburgh Journals 1767–86*, ed. Hugh M. Milne (Edinburgh: Mercat Press, 2001), p.462. Entry for 4th July, 1782.

8   John Nichol, *Inaugural Lecture to the Course of English Language and Literature, in the University of Glasgow*, Nov 17th, 1862 (Glasgow: James MacLehose, 1862), p.22.

9   The only biography is by Prof. W.A. Knight, *Memoir of John Nichol, Professor of English Literature in the University of Glasgow* (Glasgow: James MacLehose, 1896). For an up to date account see also Murray Pittock's entry on Nichol in the *New DNB*.

10 For a study of Nichol's intellectual and political miilieu, see Christopher Harvie, *The Lights of Liberalism: University Liberals and the Challenge of Democracy, 1860–1886* (London: Allen Lane, 1976).

11 Principal Shairp, *Robert Burns*, English Men of Letters (London: Macmillan, 1887). Shairp remarks of Burns's 'Holy Willy's Prayer' and other 'Kirk Satires', 'the harm they have done in Scotland is not doubtful, in that they have connected in the minds of the people so many coarse and even profane thoughts with objects which they had regarded till then with reverence.' (p.20.)

12 Quoted by Crawford, *Devolving English Literature*, pp.151.

13 Stefan Collini, *Public Moralists: Political Thought and Intellectual Life in Britain* (Oxford: Clarendon Press, 1991), p.347.

14 *English Romanticism and the Celtic World*, ed. by Gerald Carruthers and Alan Rawes (Cambridge University Press, 2003).

15 *Scotland and the Borders of Romanticism*, ed by Leith Davis, Ian Duncan, and Janet Sorensen (Cambridge University Press, 2004), p.3.

16 ibid., p.1.

17 The term 'Tartan Monster' is Tom Nairn's, and has proved controversial. See Nairn's important essay 'Old and New Scottish Nationalism', in *The Break-Up of Britain: Crisis and Neo-Nationalism*, 2nd ed., expanded (London: New Left Books, 1981), p165–8. For a critique of Nairn's argument, see Cairns Craig. *Out of History:Narrative Paradigms in Scottish and British Culture* (Edinburgh: Polygon, 1996), pp.105–112; 'what the Scotch Myths debate pointed to was not the tawdriness of Scottish culture – that was no more tawdry than any other popular culture anywhere in the world – but to the profound hatred of the intellectuals for the culture which they inhabited, the profound embarrassment they suffered by being unable, any more, to identify themselves with some universalist truth that would redeem them from Scottishness', p.107.

18 Quoted in *Scotland and Borders of Romanticism*, p.7.

19 See Christopher Harvie, 'Industry, Religion and the State of Scotland', in *The History of Scottish Literature, Vol 3., Nineteenth Century*, ed. Douglas Gifford, gen ed. Cairns Craig (Aberdeen: Aberdeen UP, 1988), p.24.

20 William Hazlitt, 'On the Scotch Character: A Fragment', in P. P. Howe, ed., *The Complete Works of William Hazlitt*, 21 volumes (London and Toronto: J.M. Dent and Sons, 1930–4), Vol 17, Uncollected Essays, p. 106.

21 Ibid., p.100.

22 William Hazlitt, ' On Burns, and the Old English Ballads', in *Lectures on the English Poets and The Spirit of the Age*, intro. by Catherine Macdonald Maclean (Dent: London: Everyman 1910), p.128 Hazlitt went on to argue, notoriously, that 'Mr Wordsworth's poetry is the

poetry of mere sentiment and pensive contemplation: Burns's is a very highly sublimated essence of animal existence.' (p.131.)

23 *Devolving English Literature*, p.18.

24 *Letters of Robert Burns*, ed. J. Lancey Ferguson, 2nd ed. by G. Ross Roy, 2 vols (Oxford: Clarendon Press, 1985), II, pp.23–4.

25 *Devolving English Literature*, p.107.

26 ibid., p.46.

27 Cairns Craig, *Out of History*, p.98.

28 ibid., p.110.

29 David Lloyd, *Nationalism and Minor Literature: James Clarence Mangan and the Emergence of Irish Cultural Nationalism* (Berkeley: University of California Press, 1987), p.77.

30 *Out of History*, p.117.

31 Susan Manning, *Fragments of Union: Making Connections in Scottish and American Writing* (Basingstoke: Palgrave, 2002), p.47.

32 *Out of History*, p.118.

33 *Robert Burns and British Poetry*, The Chatterton Lecture on Poetry, *Proceedings of the British Academy*, 121 (London: The British Academy, 2003), p.191. My thanks to Murray Pittock for a copy of his lecture.

34 [Dr James Currie] *The Works of Robert Burns; with an Account of his Life, and A Criticism on his Writings. To which are prefixed, Some Observations on the Character and Condition of the Scottish Peasantry*, 4 vols. (Liverpool, London, Edinburgh, 1800), I, pp.1–2. Henceforth *Currie* in text.

35 William Wallace Currie, *Memoir of the Life, Writing and Correspondence of James Currie, MD, FRS, of Liverpool*, 2 vols. (London: Longman, 1831), I, p.218.

36 Review of Lockhart's *Life of Burns*, *Edinburgh Review*, December 1828, in Donald Low, ed., *Robert Burns: The Critical Heritage* (London and Boston: Routledge & Kegan Paul, 1974), p.360.

37 'Resolution and Independence', in *Wordsworth: The Poems*, 3 vols., ed. John O. Hayden (Harmondsworth: Penguin, 1977), I, p.553.

38 Dorothy Wordsworth, *Recollections of a Tour Made in Scotland*, intro. notes and photographs by Carol Kyros Walker (New Haven and London: Yale University Press, 1997), p.43.

39 The 'flat sonnet' was 'This mortal body of a thousand days'. Keats' allusion in this 11–13th July 1818 journal letter to Reynolds is to *King Lear*, V iii, 17 See *Keats: The Complete Poems* (London and New York: Longman, 1970), pp.365–6.

40 'The Study of Poetry', in *Matthew Arnold: Selected Poems and Prose*, ed. Miriam Allott (London: Everyman, 1991), pp.262–3.

41 *Wordsworth: The Poems*, I, p.588, ll.33–6.

42 'Literature, Medical Science and Politics, 1795–1800: *Lyrical Ballads* and Currie's *Works of Robert Burns*', in C.C. Barfoot, *"A Natural Delineation of the Human Passions": The Historic Moment of the Lyrical Ballads* (Amsterdam and New York: Rodopi, 2003), pp.115–128.

43 Wordsworth and Coleridge, *Lyrical Ballads*, ed. by R.L. Brett and A.R. Jones, 2nd ed. (London and New York: Routledge 1991), p.7.

44 ibid., pp.245, 241.

45 See my essay 'Burns, Wordsworth, and the Politics of Vernacular Poetry' in *Land, Nation, Culture, 740–1840: Thinking the Republic of Taste*, eds., Peter de Bolla, Nigel Leask, and David Simpson (Houndmills: Palgrave Macmillan, 2005), pp.202–222.

46 *Letters of Thomas Moore*, ed Wilfred S. Dowden, 2 vols. (London: Clarendon Press, 1964), I, p.143

47 Thomas Moore, *The Life, Letters and Journals of Lord Byron*, (1830–1), New and Complete Edition, in one volume (London: John Murray, 1892), p.8.

48 ibid., p.260.

49 ibid., p.215.

50   Richard Cronin, *Romantic Victorians: English Literature, 1824–1840* (Basingstoke: Palgrave 2002), p.26.

51   Moore, *Life, Letters and Journals of Lord Byron*, p.645.

52   Hazlitt, 'On the Scotch Character: A Fragment', *Complete Works* 17, p.100.

53   Edinburgh: William Paterson 1882.

54   George Davie, *The Democratic Intellect: Scotland and her Universities in the Nineteenth Century* (Edinburgh: Edinburgh University Press, 1961), p.83.

55   John Nichol, *Inaugural Lecture*, p.15.

56   ibid., p.25.

57   ibid.

58   Andrew Hook, 'Scottish Academia and the Invention of American Studies', in Robert Crawford, (ed.), *The Scottish Invention of English Literature* (Cambridge University Press, 1998), pp.164–179.

59   Philip Hobsbaum, "A Gude Chepe Mercat of Languages": The Origin of English Teaching at Glasgow University, *College Courant*, 71 (Sept 1983), pp.10–17, p.12.

60   John Nichol, *Robert Burns*, p.67.

61   ibid., pp.6, 67.

62   Richard J. Finlay, 'The Burns Cult and Scottish Identity in the 19th and 20th Centuries', in Kenneth Simpson (ed), *Love and Liberty: Robert Burns – A Bicentenary Celebration* (East Linton: Tuckwell Press, 1997), pp.69–78; p.74.

63   *John Nichol, Robert Burns*, p.56.

64   ibid., p.2.

65   ibid., p.25.

66   ibid., p.32.

67   ibid., p.64.

68   ibid., p.4.

69   *Byron* (London: Macmillan 1880), p.18.

70   ibid.

71   ibid., p.206.

72   Quoted in Richard Finley, 'The Burns Cult', p.73. Rosebery continued; 'I use the safe adjective of British, and your applause shows me that I was right to do so', partly on the grounds that Burns himself loathed 'the use of the word English as including Scottish'. Nichol didn't share Rosebery's scruples about 'English literature'.

73   Hugh MacDiarmid, 'The Neglect of Byron' (22nd May, 1923), in *The Raucle Tongue: Hitherto Uncollected Prose*, ed. Angus Calder, Glen Murray, Alan Riach, 3 vols. (Manchester: Carcanet, 1996), I, p.77.

74   Quoted by Chris Baldick in *The Social Mission of English Criticism, 1848–1932* (Oxford: Clarendon Press, 1987), p.71.

75   Quoted by W.G. Blackie in *Remarks on the East India Company's Civil Service Examination papers; as Illustrations of some Defects in the Course of Academical Education in Scotland. Read at a meeting of the Scottish Academical Institute, Glasgow, March 4th, 1858* (Glasgow: Blackie & Co, 1858), p.1.

76   Baldick, p.71.

77   ibid., p.15.

78   ibid., p.16.

79   Nichol, *Inaugural Lecture*, p.17.

80   See Hobsbaum, p.15.

81   Knight, p.xxi.

82   See Claire Midgely's article on Pease in the *New DNB*.

83   Hobsbaum, p.12. In 1895 the Nichol Memorial Prize for the best woman student in the English Ordinary Class was inaugurated.

84   Hobsbaum, p.13.

85   Baldick, *Social Mission*, p.68.

86   John Nichol, *Scottish University Reform* (Glasgow: James MacLehose and Sons, 1888), p.36.

87   'The ignorance of Scotch affairs, which still prevails in some quarters of the south, has occasionally provoked reproachful comment', Nichol wrote, with barely concealed irony. (p.17).

88   *Scottish University Reform,* p.18.

89   John Guillory, *Cultural Capital: The Problem of Literary Canon Formation* (Chicago and London: University of Chicago Press, 1993), p.45.

90   *Scottish University Reform*, p.25. 'This year I had in one fortnight twenty excuses for non-performance of work, on the ground either of violent neuralgia, fainting, swimming in the head, or inflammation of the eyes.' Did Nichol request Doctor's letters?!

91   Ibid, p.28.

Once Upon a Time in the West of Scotland: Edwin Morgan, Modernity and Myth

Professor Alan Riach, Chair of Scottish Literature

*Inaugural Lecture delivered on 2nd December 2006
in the Sir Charles Wilson Theatre, Glasgow University*

Once Upon a Time . . .

I want to begin by recollecting a misty October evening in Cambridge, many years ago, where I'm approaching a lecture theatre to hear a talk by the West Indian novelist Wilson Harris. It is an obscure and ghostly night. The lighting is dim. The air seems haunted. The speaker on the stage is unassuming and begins in a quiet voice, telling us that we all know how sometimes people rise up from the pages of history to confront the authorities who seek to control them, and he mentioned how people under the communist regimes of eastern Europe were rising against a system that had closed down on them, and how the consumers of capitalism might also confront the heartless intrusions of advertising. Authors, too, he said, are sometimes confronted by their creations. And he told us how, a few days before, Aunt Alicia, one of the characters from his novel *The Four Banks of the River of Space*, had appeared in his study and torn into shreds the lecture he had carefully prepared to deliver that night.

We noted that he had only a few fragments of notes in front of him.

'No,' she had said to him. 'No carefully-prepared lecture for you,' she said. 'Tonight you must talk from the depths of your vulnerability.'[1]

Well, I have prepared my lecture as best I can but I would like to assure you I feel very much as though I am speaking from the depths of my vulnerability this afternoon.

What emerged from that moment in Cambridge was a strange realisation of something that was never spoken or explicitly stated at the time. Here, in the centre of the most privileged educational institution, was an author speaking from a history and out of a location which that privilege had, for generations, kept to the margins of literary attention. Here was not only an author but a subject, one of those people who might rise up to confront their judges with judgements of his own. And I think from that moment I began to sense more deeply the relationship which Wilson Harris himself had drawn attention to long before, between the literatures of the world arising in the wake of the Anglophone empire, and the literature of Scotland.

This was a critical and historical consideration, a review of how literature and culture might be read and understood. But it was also a creative act, an intervention in the status quo. It was a twofold impetus, a doubled focus. Part of it demanded reading literary history through new and different lenses; part of it demanded new writing.

What I have to say this afternoon begins with that sense of doubleness, a sense that literary scholarship, historical description and theoretical analysis, is always and always necessarily connected reciprocally to a creativity that is the provenance of original artists. This might be an obvious enough point, simply to say, good reading and good writing are mutual, strengthening. The further one leaves the other behind the worse each becomes. Yet the obvious is often the most easily overlooked. And there is a particular emphasis that I want to insist upon, that this understanding is deeply realised from the originary moment of modernity in Scottish literature.

Where are we to locate that moment? One might argue, *waaaay back*, in 1603, when the late medieval Elizabethan world switched to early modern Jacobean, when the Scottish King James the Saxt became the First of the two United Kingdoms, and Shakespeare wrote his greatest tragedies. Would Elizabeth have permitted *Lear*?

But I'm straying too deep.

Not so far back then, 1707 and what ensued: the creation of English rhetoric, belles-lettres, a disposition towards the language of speculative thought that distanced itself from speech. The legacy of the carefulness of Enlightenment English was an anti-Scots bias that favoured exclusively English diction and the supremacy of the English language in writing. The Scots language was relegated to the status of dialect and is currently considered by many people to be no more than 'slang'. Yet the long reach of Enlightenment English ultimately delivers the goods in the language of the poetry of Norman MacCaig, where it returns to the precisions of speech. No contemporary English-language poetry is more sensitively attuned to the cadences of the spoken tongue and the liabilities of what seems to be linguistic definition.

Yet in the full spectrum of Scotland's voices, MacCaig's perfect pitch is both separate from, and connected to, the Scots vernacular of another, parallel tradition. The vernacular is what Ramsay, Fergusson and Burns enacted; it was the ideal to which Wordsworth aspired in his time, as Ezra Pound in his, it was what Hugh MacDiarmid, William Soutar and Lewis Grassic Gibbon possessed in theirs, Tom Leonard and Liz Lochhead in ours. And after all, as that paradigm of Enlightenment subversion David Hume reminds us, it is pleasure that reason is there to serve and teaching only really works by its virtue. As William Carlos Williams puts it, 'If it ain't a pleasure, it ain't a poem!' But this false distinction – between vernacular Scots and Enlightened English, between animal instinct and intellectuality and reason, between, on the one hand, Burns's jolly beggars and the women of Tony Roper's play *The Steamie*, and, on the other, those of us who have had the unquestionable benefits of education through to tertiary level – this distinction has bedevilled modern Scotland in a way it never did in Ireland or America.

Its antidote was there in MacDiarmid and it stays with us, a deep resource, in the trajectory that takes us from him to Morgan. However, through that trajectory, in education, the legacy for Scottish modernity of the ascendancy of English is a much less triumphant story and I'll be coming back to that.

But let's start modernity – or the myth of modernity – once upon a time in the 1880s. James Thomson has just published *The City of Dreadful Night*. Introducing a 1993 edition of this great poem, Edwin Morgan says this:

> [For Thomson,] The whole change of environment from Scotland to (say) London – the complex of physical, cultural, linguistic changes – may also have forced, under pressure of various kinds, new ways of looking at things, a new awareness of things that an outsider suddenly sees and points out. T.S. Eliot's published tribute to both Thomson and Davidson . . . was that they had a particular kind of modernity . . . which he did not find in their English contemporaries . . . [They were] symbolic of the exile and alienation of the early-modern artist.[2]

It's that double thrust again, the critical revaluation of the poetry of the past and its vitality as a source for new writing, the writing Eliot himself would produce in 1922, in *The Waste Land*, through Ezra Pound's red pen and a startling poetics of fragment-narratives and an ear tuned into the musical phrase. Whether Shakespeare in a London at the beginning of colonial expansion, or Thomson and Davidson in a London at the end of the era of Anglocentric empire, the critical imagination engages with displacement and discontinuity creatively and actively. Critical reappraisal, creative practice. Understanding and acting.

But these are preliminaries, only. Rehearsals.

The moment we begin with really, the originary moment of modernity in Scottish literature, is MacDiarmid.

In the early 1920s MacDiarmid devised two slogans which are now familiar enough but I'd like to rehearse them again, to read them wilfully to yield two contradictory but complimentary meanings which if MacDiarmid didn't fully explain, he implicitly sanctioned. At least they give his latent authority for the complementarity of scholarship and creativity and they summarise what I've been indicating.

'Not Burns – Dunbar!' might be read as a call to re-establish long traditions of neglected literary and cultural history, to revalue the full inherited file. And 'Not traditions – precedents!' suggests that as creative artists, poets, thinkers, critics, whoever we are, you take what you want from anywhere, to create, you abandon traditional definitions or constraints and seize the initiatives that can be put to creative use. One represents an impulse towards categorical knowledge, comprehensive understanding, codification and securities; the other represents spontaneity – not in the total abandonment of form but in a different, unpredicted habitation of it. One might be embodied by scholarship, the other by artistry.[3]

Scotland, like anywhere else, may be cursed and possessed by the worst exaggerations of either in extremes: the mortmain of weighted pedantry (so to speak) or the emptiness of mere gesture. The tedium of solemnity and the tiresomeness of vandalism are equally dangerous forms of delusion. Yet the closure canonicity may seem to threaten is always open to revision when the impulse to subversion remains as essential as the recognition of the authority of co-ordinates. It would be a mistake to be locked into one or the other posture: either active in the constant subversion of canonicity or fixed in support of a perpetually unchanging canon. Both positions are false promises of stability.

It is a commonplace now to describe the key change in perception made in the modern era as 'The Moment of Cubism'. John Berger's famous essay is neatly condensed in the sentence from his novel *G.* that 'No story can be told now as if it were the only story.'[4] I'm well aware that the story I'm going to tell has happened in a world of intersecting stories, trajectories that overlap or cut across the one I want to emphasise. Still it seems to me worth briefly rehearsing the way in which the Scottish Renaissance movement, and MacDiarmid especially, took as its new beginning a deliberate attempt to reclaim a lost past, an abandoned history. To go back to go forward, to reclaim the ballad, Dunbar, the lost Scotland described in MacDiarmid's 'Homage to Dunbar':

> Wha wull may gang to Scott's or Burns's grave
> But nane to yours, in your lost Scotland, lost
> Neth this oor Scotland as neth the ocean wave
> Atlantis lies, and haud'n a greater host . . .
>
> Still, like the bells o' Ys frae unplumbed deeps,
> Whiles through Life's drumlie wash your music leaps
> To'n antrin ear, as a'e bird's wheep defines
> In some lane place the solitude's outlines . . . [5]

For Edwin Morgan, forty years after MacDiarmid's first struggles, the empowerment towards the new came from a similar balance of national and international sources. The pressurised stability of his own biography was counterbalanced by the variety and volume of translations, on the one hand, and on the other, the liberation of American poetics in the tide of the Beat, Black Mountain and San Francisco poets, brought together so effectively by Donald Allen in his seminal 1960 anthology *The New American Poetry*.[6] In fact, the American poets were welcomed to Scotland before that, in a 1959 essay from the Edinburgh University students' magazine *Jabberwock*, 'America's Example to Scottish Writers':

> Whether or not we consolidate the experiments of Hart Crane and e.e. cummings is largely irrelevant since while we are busy 'consolidating,' a brand new 'English' literature will be appearing in Johannesburg or Sydney or Vancouver or Madras (or even Edinburgh!) . . .
>
> It is in this spirit that I welcome the appearance here [in Scotland] of Robert Creeley, Allen Ginsberg, Charles Olson, Philip Whalen, Michael McClure, and the other American creative artists.[7]

It is salutary to note that these words were written by MacDiarmid himself in 1959. What's noteworthy I think is not only that he's welcoming the American writers but that he's connecting them with the rising postcolonial literatures in English – in South Africa, Australia, Canada, India, or indeed Scotland – which will achieve prominence in the next decade – Chinua Achebe's *Things Fall Apart* had been published just the year before – and that in this context of border-crossings, international shadow lines, transgressions of all sorts, Scottish poets had much to learn. Edwin Morgan did exactly that.

And it's the same lesson: the leap of an unpredicted music from the depths or distances where solitude is outlined. Here is Morgan's instamatic snapshot from 'NIGERIA UNDATED REPORTED OCTOBER 1971':

> An Englishman in a Land Rover driving north
> has reached the Niger. A sign says
> HALT. NO PHOTOGRAPHS. He gets out,
> climbs a steep slope, and suddenly
> there is the black narrow iron bridge
> against the sky, but it is not blue
> shows through, but milky white,
> the slow close gentle steady ripple
> of hundreds of white cattle
> bound for Lagos market,
> making every bar and strand and spar and iron star
> stand out in living art,
> a moving and unmoving caterpillar
> bristled with sticks of herd-boys,
> feeding high in air
> above the huge brown river.
> A white plinth on the bank
> like some great animal's cast tooth
> marks
> Mungo Park.[8]

MacDiarmid and Morgan: both shared this double practice. Now, looking back over their almost completed works, you can see them, both in their ways, teacher and poet, pedagogues, the original 'Informationists', each with a deeply politicised social vision of what the place might be; poets concerned with a better quality of reading, and so with education, and the context of Scottish literature in which their works might best be read.[9]

The Edwin Morgan Centre for Creative Writing here at Glasgow University arose partly in fulfilment of Morgan's example, but it's worth reminding ourselves of the sensitivity such practice requires. In 1959, Morgan's view on creative writing at universities was loud and lucid: 'I am opposed to the American experiment of complete rationalisation of the creative writer's position and function within the universities, because it has produced . . . a generation of technically advanced and professionally cultivated poets . . . whose response to life itself has atrophied and whose poetry is impotent to move and inspire the human heart.'[10]

There's a cautionary tone there but it serves to remind us that the 'merely professional' is never enough. The increasing popularity and strong tradition of creative writing goes from strength to strength at Glasgow by remembering this – it can never be formulaic. What it makes possible is access to the risks that joy insists on. Or to paraphrase Nietzsche, chaos is *required*, or there are no dancing stars.[11]

There was no doubt about Morgan's commitment to balancing the two aspects of his own work. For MacDiarmid, what Scotland needed was not more writers so much as more good readers. Indeed, it was the critics of Scottish literature with whom MacDiarmid found most fault in the 1920s, not the perpetrators of primary texts. 'Scottish literature,' he wrote in 1922, 'like all other literatures, has been *written* almost exclusively by blasphemers, immoralists, dipsomaniacs, and madmen, but, unlike most other literatures, it has been *written about* almost exclusively by ministers . . . '[12]

This distancing is usefully devalued by Bertolt Brecht: 'Bourgeois philosophers make a distinction between the active man and the reflective man. The thinking man draws no such distinction.'[13] I'd like to keep that in mind as a central principle informing the work and lives of both MacDiarmid and Morgan.

Perhaps one virtue of the marketplace used to be that it was a central social location where people from different languages and cultures might meet and barter and talk to each other, as people did in the old town of Edinburgh, and still do in Glasgow even now. Today, though, there's a new problem. Distinctions are drawn more tightly. The market has developed with technology to such a degree that 'target audiences' might be addressed exclusively so that the commerce between readerships is critically limited for a maximum sell. The wide and general address is itself therefore being broken up.

It's the old story – divide and rule – nowhere more evident than in Scotland's story and countered by the work of our greatest writers. But now it's a globalised story. I don't need to emphasise the relevance this has for ideals of the democratic intellect and in legislative terms, for the four-year Scottish general degree – or that a poet might write for non-specialists. Nor is this simply an opposition between our work and 'media' – the equivalent of advertising's 'target audiences' is academia's bad jargon and 'narrow specialisms' (and RAE priorities tell us how defining and delimiting they can be).

Earlier this afternoon, Nigel spoke eloquently about 'border crossings' and the renewable value of tracking proximities and connections across the shadow lines, the debatable lands of history and literary tradition. What I've just said endorses Nigel's recognition of the fertile ground of border crossings. But I guess what I'm saying now to complement that is that the shadow lines are not enough. To cross them, we're moving from one place to another, and however subtly the spectrum alters, however imperceptibly we might dwell in the land 'between', our job is to speak about the things unspoken, to debate the debatable lands. And to do that, we need to know more about our own place.

I'd like to move out from that populous, actively moving area of the borderlands for a few minutes and just think a little about what you might take to be at the furthest extreme from it, the area of exile. It is, after all, a key trope of modernity. Conrad, Joyce, Eliot, Pound – so many of the key figures of the era were exiles, and no less were Thomson and Davidson in London, Lewis Grassic Gibbon in Welwyn Garden City and MacDiarmid in Shetland.

When I went to New Zealand in 1986, on a one-year post-doctoral fellowship, I knew nobody and had no idea what I was getting into. I was crossing more than one shadow line, flying over numerous 'risky horizons' – and that phrase comes from a poem written to commemorate the 300th anniversary of the discovery of New Zealand (as it were) by Abel Tasman, on 13 December 1642, 'Landfall in Unknown Seas' by Allen Curnow:

> Well, home is the sailor, and that is a chapter
> In a schoolbook, a relevant yesterday
> We thought we knew all about, being much apter
> To profit, sure of our ground,
> No murderers mooring in our Golden Bay.

> But now there are no more islands to be found
> And the eye scans risky horizons of its own
> In unsettled weather, and murmurs of the drowned
> Haunt their familiar beaches –
> Who navigates us towards what unknown

But not impossible provinces? Who reaches
A future down for us from the high shelf
Of spiritual destiny?[14]

Curnow's poem from 1942 reminds us precisely of the co-
ordinates the world provides for our subject. Its connection with
Scotland is distant but tenacious, that opening reference to
Stevenson's 'Requiem' instantly recognisable but also almost
forgotten, 'a relevant yesterday' or 'a chapter/In a schoolbook'.
The connection of New Zealand and Scotland is tangible, therefore, not only in that haunting use of citation but in the most
literal sense of human, generational contact across geographical
distance. Scotland relates to modernity in the work of such 'exiles'
whose writing is so carefully attuned both to national identity and
to the 'murmurs' and hauntings, the drowned voices reminiscent
of Eliot's distant songs emerging from exhausted wells.[15] Along
with James K. Baxter, Curnow is New Zealand's first great national
poet, but Curnow – and Baxter even more so – endorse their
national identity by specific reference to the Scotland that attaches
to them, that haunts and murmurs to them yet. Literally, as Pound
noted, we do not all live in the same time, there are different speeds
in it, different velocities.[16]

When I returned from New Zealand, fourteen years later, I arrived
back in Scotland in January 2001. I phoned my immediate employer,
Douglas Gifford, the night I arrived and he told me he knew that
I'd probably be jet-lagged so I should take the following morning
off. Douglas, I have to take this opportunity to thank you publicly
for all the generosities, personal and professional, you've shown to
Rae and me over the last six years.

First of many was showing me where to catch the bus to the

university. I was back in the vernacular idiom of Scotland: normality. Burns, MacDiarmid, Morgan – as opposed to the risky horizons I'd crossed in New Zealand.

So I'm just arrived from the golden sands and freshly-laundered waves of New Zealand's glorious midsummer and it's 7 o'clock in the morning in a pitch-black perishing January in Ayr and I'm waiting for the bus Douglas has informed me will go straight through to the university. Lights move along the tree-lined road through the whistling wind and the bus pulls up. I get on board and ask for a ticket. 'Sorry, pal,' my driver says, 'the bus you want's the university bus – ' and as we speak the university bus is overtaking us and driving past us, on into the early morning dark.

'It's okay,' says my driver. 'Sit doon. We'll get'm!'

And we're off, through the silent streets of Ayr, the big stone houses on either side like manses, curtains drawn, no traffic, as my driver races up behind the bus in front – these two long single-decker buses, with the bendy elastic band in the middle, and it's like that film, *Speed*, until my driver screeches out to overtake the bus in front, pulls in in front of him diagonally cutting across the whole road and blocking it completely.

'On ye go pal,' he cries triumphantly. 'He's no' gonny get oot o' that!'

Home.

It's that deep sense of residence. Inhabitation. The idea that in fact, you *can* go home, the return to an earth that will never, really, let us leave. Whatever I understand about literature must owe something to that sense of what makes being in a place worthwhile. And that is partly the virtue of acquiring the sense of being so far away from 'belonging' that all you are left with are the 'risky horizons' at 'the world's end where wonders cease.'[17]

For me, Scottish literature and my own poetry were two things that focused while I was in New Zealand – two things that were essential to what I want to be concerned with. When I left in 1986, I left all the poems I'd written behind, deciding that if they mattered I'd know in a month or two, or otherwise I should let that practice go. It took a month or so. I knew I was going to have to go back to them. I phoned my parents and asked them to pull out the box under the desk and send it to me, please. Some things you cannot do without, and at the end of that first year Auckland University Press published the first book, *This Folding Map*, and Oxford University Press published it in Britain.

Meanwhile through the 1980s and 1990s a massive revaluation of Scottish literature and other arts was taking place. The books by Roderick Watson, Cairns Craig, Douglas Gifford, Duncan Macmillan's work on Scottish art, John Purser's work on Scotland's music – from the distance of New Zealand, these and many others helped bring about a critical context in which Scotland could not be confined to the catalogue of clichés and caricatures so familiar to us all. And I think that Marshall Walker's *Scottish Literature Since 1707* and my own work on MacDiarmid contributed valuably to that context as well.[18]

That reapproachment, that bringing together, that movement in a place where extremes might meet, yields matter that sometimes might seem wild, but in time, might be productive. I went to New Zealand partly on the strength of curiosity out of reading Herman Melville, the book with the map. My father gave me my first copy of *Moby-Dick* for Christmas when I was fourteen. It took my breath away.

I am very lucky that my mother and father are here today and I would like to say thank you, to both of you. I am proud of you.

Working on MacDiarmid's uncollected essays while in New Zealand, I remember turning up his wild claim that *Moby-Dick* in fact was the greatest of all Scottish novels.[19] An accident of ancestry? An affinity of themes or tones? Whatever it was MacDiarmid wanted from it, Melville's masterpiece has not, so far, been claimed by Scottish literature. Yet reading *The Melville Log*, the biography began to yield for me a character whose own deep sense of what ancestral longing and belonging had to offer moved him literally, actually, to make his own extended visit to Scotland.[20] This was something I knew, something I wanted to articulate in my own way. This is 'Melville in Glasgow':

Consider it a sketch: charcoal on grain, white paper, black ash,
clouds and the Necropolis, the perfect size and shape of that Cathedral,
to see it from the south side of the Clyde and think of modesty
    and reach, the country all around; to think of what was there, and
    what
that man was looking for, a past that might say more than all the risk
he'd known before he stepped up on that quay: what did he want?
A family? A line? A net? A country? A link in a chain he couldn't put
    down,
to haul up something far too deeply rusted out of sight; yet not too far:
he knew it was there, went looking for it, crossed the country, walked
    and rode and
came back in to Glasgow: his place, his port. The first and last he saw,
    of some-
thing then he must have thought ancestral, real as all the things he knew
    had happened
to him, in the South Pacific, visceral, in blood and muscle, yielding to
    delight,
yet also always fictional: build on that. On what? Where was he then?
What strength and what uncertainty, and what desire to know, dared
    push that pen?[21]

The most far-flung thing and the nearest things – the night sky, stars and islands of a very distant hemisphere – and the eye and breath and voices of a place I'd always know as home. This was what MacDiarmid was asking us to pay attention to. And in a similar way, a generation later, it's Morgan's prerogative also. Find out what's on the periphery, move it to the centre. See how it changes the scene. Turn the kaleidoscope, twist the colours round.

In New Zealand we had a visit from the President of Ireland, Mary Robinson. The line she delivered has haunted me ever since. 'The arts are the genius of your country,' she said. 'And education is the key with which you unlock the door.'

Is this an accumulating argument for more Departments of Scottish Literature? How far can we countenance – culturally, educationally, not to mention politically – the prospect of autonomy?

MacDiarmid's answer is refreshingly forthright. The poem is called 'Separatism':

> If there's a sword-like sang
> That can cut Scotland clear
> O' a' the warld beside
> Rax me the hilt o't here.
>
> For there's nae jewel till
> Frae the rest o' earth it's free,
> Wi' the starry separateness
> I'd fain to Scotland gie.[22]

The worst implications of exceptionalism are challenged here by the dazzling appeal of language and metaphor (both the energy of

'Rax' and the beauty of 'starry separateness' are verbally persuasive beyond the clod-bound correctnesses that mundane politics insists upon). Again, the continuity may be felt in the vision of an independent and self-determined nation in which there is room for difference and dialogue and no enforcement of sterile uniformity.

The continuity from MacDiarmid to Morgan is clear. If the poem I just quoted appears to endorse a crystalline uniqueness, an absolute exceptionalism that would be very suspect after the claims to ultimate supremacy made disgustingly familiar by Nazi ideology and more recent claims to fundamentalist exceptionalism, we should bear in mind that the human urge towards self-definition need not be tainted by such horrors. MacDiarmid also wrote the lines taken by that most sceptical, curious and optimistic of 1980s journals, *Cencrastus*, as its motto – 'If there is anything worthwhile in Scotland now, there is no distance to which it's unattached' – in other words, all the self-determination in the world can only be valuable if it's kept in touch with everything else, a healthy self-extension into all the far-flung corners, the peripheries, margins, the places beyond history – 'If there is ocht in Scotland that's worth hae'in'/There is nae distance tae which it's unattached!'[23]

Separateness and connectedness. It's that doubleness again.

A specific example. The more eclectic amongst us this afternoon will have recognised that the title of my lecture comes from Sergio Leone's magnificent spaghetti western of 1968. I thought it appropriate partly because of a line delivered by Clint Eastwood in the first of the Leone movies that led up to *Once Upon a Time in the West*. Arriving at the border town of San Miguel – a town positively crepuscular with shadow lines! – the Man with No Name encounters the two warring family-clans who live in their big houses at either end of the main street. In the middle of the street the saloon-keeper befriends him, and he takes his chance to go upstairs onto the balcony of the saloon to take an overview of the situation. 'Things look different from higher up,' he explains. Well, the inaugural lecture from the Chair of Scottish Literature ought to be able to take a look at things from higher up.

There's another reason for the title, as well as the literal indication towards Edwin Morgan, whose work in the west of Scotland at this university I'll come back to. It's a vicarious pleasure to have the opportunity to evoke the image of my grandfather, Papa, my mother's father, a twelve-year old boy in 1911, being taken by his parents to the Kelvingrove Empire Exhibition and, sixty-odd years later, telling me how much he'd enjoyed the stagecoach battle in Buffalo Bill's Wild West Show. This was part of an exhibition which generated funds that, along with money from various other donors, helped to establish the first Chair of Scottish History and Literature in the following year. The initiative seems to have come from Principal Donald McAllister, a physician, born in Perth, a native Gaelic speaker, who attended Cambridge University in 1877 and was Principal of Glasgow University from 1907 till 1929. It was through his encouragement and investment that the Chair of Scottish History and Literature was established.[24]

Once upon a time in the west of Scotland . . .

And it's very important to see how the establishment of the Chair and the Department of Scottish Literature developed out of Scottish history, not from English Literature. The subject of Scottish history dominated the study of our literature and until quite recently it was impossible to study Scottish literature without studying Scottish history as well. Professors appointed were: Sir Robert Rait (1913) – who later became Principal of this University – J.D. Mackie (1930), G.S. Pryde (1957), Archibald Alexander McBeth Duncan (1962) and Edward J. Cowan (1994), then in 1995 Professor Douglas Gifford was appointed to the first separate single Glasgow University-established Chair of Scottish Literature, though the Department had been established in 1971 and was led at that time by Alexander Scott then by Roderick Lyall before Douglas Gifford and now myself. So the development of the subject in the University dovetailed the establishment of the Chair and the Department.

See this, for a moment, against the background of the longer term: late eighteenth-century university courses in English, Rhetoric and Belles-Lettres segue into courses in English Literature and the establishment of Chairs in that subject from the 1860s to the 1890s, tearing the emphasis away from Classical Studies to appreciation of English literature and history. American literary studies follow: Henry S. Salt began his 1892 obituary of Herman Melville in *The Gentleman's Magazine* with the question, 'Has America a literature?' For him, American literature was grand and chaotic with a brilliant but suppressed imagination.[25]

Similar in its description of a kind of cultural personality that was undefined, reckless, extreme, vivid, open to facts as much as elfland, was G. Gregory Smith's 1919 *Scottish Literature: Character and Influence*.[26] And after World War II, we're familiar with the rise of Irish and then Commonwealth and 'postcolonial' literary studies. All these subject areas have their own little empires of authority, hierarchies of power, favoured authorities, places and people.

And Scottish Literature?

Well, as we've noted, the study of the subject had its genesis in history – and that provides a valuable sense of chronology – a spine – it's a vertebrate subject – and the legacy of that is still very much the governing principle of how our teaching is structured in the Department. But something else is in play. The academic study of the subject is immersed in the context of the writers who are creating it. This is the point I said I'd come back to about Edwin Morgan's surreptitious smuggling into courses ostensibly in English Literature, not only of current writing from America – his introduction of Allen Ginsberg's 'Howl' remains a talking-point – but also of Scottish Literature, and his friendship and encouragement of Alexander Scott, not only the first Head of my Department but a fine poet and playwright himself.

One frequent student response is the real pleasure to discover that you're walking around among the people you're studying, meeting them, talking to them. I am delighted to have helped to appoint Liz Lochhead to the current Writer-in-Residency and it was unforgettable when Edwin Morgan encountered our first-year students in succeeding years at the beginning of the current millennium.

So the spine of tradition and the chaotic presence of writers who are unpredicted – this clearly tracks back to MacDiarmid's double impetus I mentioned at the beginning of the lecture, and forward through Morgan's practice as poet and teacher, on into the present and future.

Literature works *between* history and theory – it cannot be reduced to evidence, data, archaeology and documentary, nor can it be subsumed into ideology, religious orthodoxy, theoretical abstraction. Literature is evidence but it's also more than that. Literature is part of the ideology of its politics, place and time, but it is also more than that. It arises from the matter of history, the facts and forms and lives of people in their own times and places, and it interrogates the assumptions that surround us, actively, aggressively sometimes. In cultures where answers are prescribed and questions proscribed, its value is high and dangerous. Increasingly, as dogma, doctrine, persuasion and selling dominate the air, its questions are devalued and its functions marginalised. It cannot be contained and defined by the past, as history. Nor will the best of it be accommodated by market fashions and vogue. *Moby-Dick* was a very unpopular book, in its time. But it *will* survive *despite* the foreclosures of the orthodox.

Remember Edwin Morgan's 'Demon' poems?

> My job is to rattle the bars. It's a battle.
> The gates are high, large, long, hard, black.
> Whatever the metal is, it is asking to be struck.
> There are guards of course, but I am very fast
> And within limits I can change my shape.
> The dog watches me, but I am not trying
> To get out, nor am I trying to get in.
> He growls if I lift my iron shaft.
> I smile at that, and with a sudden whack
> I drag it lingeringly and resoundingly
> Along the gate; then he's berserk: fine![27]

The Demon is the cure when tranquillity turns to complacency. The Demon is a vitalising spirit, real and living in us. A literary education helps us read the world more richly, critically, neither resting on the securities of historical foundations nor acquiescing easily in the platitudinous orthodoxies of the status quo. If all poets are of the Devil's party, so are all good readings.

Scottish literature goes further and deeper into the past, literally, than any of the postcolonial literatures, simply by historical definition. How could anyone objectively purport to know the extent and value of our literature, when the National Library of Scotland, the Mitchell Library in Glasgow, our own University Library, are so full of archival material, even now, under-researched.

I am therefore compelled to argue that there should be an established Chair of Scottish Literature in each one of the universities in Scotland, whose primary responsibility would be to teach and research in the subject area, to safeguard and promote the subject.

How curious that this does not already pertain!

As professional scholars, our expertise is rewarded by personal promotion to senior positions. But personal professorships, however committed the person, are at the mercy of financial imperatives, and in the climate of Research Assessment, headhunting and 'accountability', being bought and sold for, well, somebody's gold, is a familiar story.

So, an established Chair in every Scottish university.

More than that.

I can imagine very reasonable arguments coming from my friends and colleagues, very sensible discussions agreeing that it's very good that Scotland has a Department of Scottish Literature at Glasgow University but really, there's no need for every university in Scotland to have one, is there? Of course, of course, and pass the Tio Pepe.

Wrong.

Let's imagine a different world. There is a Department of Scottish Literature in all Scottish universities, working alongside and in collaboration with English, in literature and language, and other literatures and closely with Departments whose responsibilities equally are to all the other areas of cultural production in Scotland as they are taught – theatre, art, music, film, television, radio and with history. Each Department is also staffed with an artist, composer, writer-in-residence and each area of cultural production is fully equipped to drive back into history, from Morgan through MacDiarmid, past Burns and Jean Elliott to Dunbar and Columba; from Peter Howson and Ken Currie through Joan Eardley and the Scottish Colourists and the Glasgow Boys and Girls to Wilkie and Raeburn and further; from James Macmillan and Judith Weir through Ronald Stevenson and F.G. Scott to John Blackwood McEwan, Hamish MacCunn, right back to Robert Carver.

To those who argue, reasonably, so much depends upon personalities – academics are so protective, jealously guarding their areas – the answer is yes, and that's precisely why you need institutional investment in the subject.

Only by such institutional investment will we secure the provision in universities which can give potential schoolteachers a grounding in Scottish literature and the arts which they can then take with them into the schools. Without that, generations will continue to suffer prejudice, dullness and ignorance. Some time ago, school pupils were required to answer a compulsory exam question on Scottish literature, in recognition of the fact that the only way to ensure that people study the subject is to assess it. Currently, Scottish literature is one among many options in literary studies in schools. That status is not good enough.

I said that I'd come back to the long legacy of the ascendancy of English since the Enlightenment, the grimmest aspect of our story. If that legacy is found in the urge to categorise knowledge, codify language and quantify product, its current effects are increasingly unwelcome.

I went to talk to a hundred schoolteachers in Grangemouth a week ago. They'd spent the morning filling in their forms, responsibly responding to the bureaucracy that seems to employ them, a morning spent on 'accountability' – and to me, they all seemed desperately keen for what I could give them, simply about what modern Scottish poetry can do. When most of your money is spent on protecting the thing, and not on the thing you're protecting, you're wasting your money. In Greenock, a couple of years ago, I had the chance to introduce another group of schoolteachers to W.S. Graham, born there at 1 Hope Street, and his unforgettable poem, 'Loch Thom'. Reading that poem with them brought me back to the point of all the arts. They're there to help people to live.

The great Scottish artist and teacher William Johnstone noted that 'It is idle to blame teachers. My criticism of educational methods is aimed at certain consequences of the prevalent attitude to experience.'[28]

However, the prevalent attitude to experience today compounds a long tradition of condescension and under-valuation of Scottish literature, language and art which has prevailed for generations, spawned in the Enlightenment and fostered by the Empire.

Scots didn't 'invent' English literature but if we helped to create English literary studies, in the long term with regard to our own educational system, it was an 'own-goal' and nothing to be pleased about.

Have our universities fully served our schoolteachers? Has our government served the universities? Surely, today, universities are more than ever required to be visibly accountable to the government and, therefore, to the taxpayer, to the people?

Let me offer a general observation. These words are by Professor Marshall Walker, formerly of the university where I used to teach in New Zealand:

The impression that the university belongs to the people is false for two reasons. First, under thrall to Ministry of Education committees it is in the process of becoming government property. Second, it is less than a university in exact proportion to the extent to which it belongs to the government and therefore lacks academic freedom. The nature of the institution as it is now evolving is that of a clumsily government-controlled nonuniversity in a condition of bureaucratic entropy. Accountability *sounds* responsible – the word tintinnabulates with high moral tone – but *means* that academics are increasingly required to turn their attention from teaching, learning and research, to immerse themselves in administration and spend their time not in the laboratory or the class-room or the study or the library but in composing mission statements, reports and projections, in committees, in number-crunching and in trying to keep afloat in an unebbing ocean of [electronic] memoranda. The more academics are so deflected from freely studying and teaching their subjects the less entitled the institution is to call itself a university.[29]

Let me return to Glasgow. The situation is familiar enough. Here and now we are enmeshed in a culture where competition insists upon a constant bidding for resources, specifically for research funding, in an air verbally saturated with the language of corporatese, developed in the context of commercialism. The words seem stale already, as if knowledge, experience, wisdom and acts were market commodities, instead of the matter and movement in which you spend your life.

Some systems bring out the good in people, some bring out the worst. The problem is a long way from solution.

If MacDiarmid's response to injustice was outspoken, often outrageously explicit polemic, Morgan's example is different. Subtle, sustained, subversive, but no less determined, steely and, at its core, equally resistant to the vicissitudes of diversion and decoy bad management always brings upon us. And this is the virtue of poetry: it is applicable. Just as his love poetry is love poetry, not to be confined to any single disposition, so his William Blake-like declaration of intent, 'The Fifth Gospel', goes further than any specific location, but surely prefigures the messages he has given us with increasingly terse intensity in the most recent years of his life, when he has known he has no time to spare. Look at the opening lines of his poem about William Wallace from 2005, which was prompted by Lesley Duncan of *The Herald*, and which he himself was surprised to find was written with such speed and passion:

> Surely it is better to forget.
> It is better not to forget.[30]

Or the lines from the trilogy of plays on the life of Christ, *A.D.*, which managed to challenge the orthodoxies of both sectarian ends of the spectrum of our perpetually clashing armies of eternal cultural night. Morgan, revising the familiar liturgical formula, vitalises our sense of what our business is for:

> In the midst of life I find myself in art.
> In the midst of art I find myself in life.[31]

And back in 1973, in 'The Fifth Gospel', he set the hunt that tracks us, even now:

I have come to overthrow the law and the prophets: I have not come to fulfil, but to overthrow . . .

It is not those that are sick who need a doctor, but those that are healthy. I have not come to call sinners, but the virtuous and law-abiding, to repentance . . .

Give nothing to Caesar, for nothing is Caesar's.[32]

The great triumph of the story of modern Scottish literary criticism – the goal and examples set by MacDiarmid and Morgan – is evident, from Maurice Lindsay's little pamphlet of 1947 and Sydney Goodsir Smith's wee booklet of 1951 to Douglas Gifford's *vade mecum* of 1200-odd pages of 2002, and the new *Edinburgh History of Scottish Literature*. From last Tuesday morning, the 835-page *Alba Literaria: A History of Scottish Literature*, edited and introduced by Marco Fazzini, the first comprehensive book of its kind entirely planned and produced outside of Scotland, from Italy; and last Wednesday, the two-volume history of *The Literature of Scotland* by Roderick Watson. Three major new accounts arriving in the last week! And only last Thursday, St Andrew's Day, the Literature Forum and the Saltire Society Book Awards. It has been a phenomenal week![33]

Signals, signs.

Yet how can it be that it is still perfectly possible for a boy or girl to go through their entire school-life and emerge with no knowledge at all of Scottish literature, art or classical music?

How can it be possible that a child growing up in Scotland might go through primary, secondary and, yes, specialising in literature, tertiary education too, and meet with none of the literature of the country he or she resides in?

The need is clear, for supporting strengths between good critical journalism, literary criticism, imaginative writing, historical understanding, the university teaching of Scottish literature and theoretical considerations – all these different forms of good reading. A much greater degree of institutional investment in the subjects and their inter-relatedness than they have ever had, is required now. After all, the job of politicians is always no more than to help sustain an economy in which the arts can flourish and people can benefit from

them. Everything else in politics is merely distraction. In the review of
the schools' so-called 'Curriculum for Excellence' and the development
of a dialogue with the prescribing authorities, I have seen how difficult it sometimes is to insist on the fact that all forms of Scottish
cultural production through the centuries need to be visible, vital,
present. Perhaps Scottish literature will always have to be fought for.

Perhaps it is precisely the multiplicity of forms and genres, languages
and voices, such a range of kinds of experience demanding their own
literary expressions, that constitutes in itself the defining character-
istic of Scottish literature. It's because we require the whole inherited file and need the doors kept open – watertight compartments
are only good for sinking ships – that MacDiarmid and Morgan
remain exemplary in their openness.

And the open complexity of all human experience is precisely the
domain of the arts. And understanding this is – and remains – a
form of resistance.

It is to resist the vanity of all efforts to bind and contain imaginative life. It is to resist the mechanical excess of systematic meaning.
It is to teach that intelligence and sensitivity reside with an irreducible
openness, never with the closed.

In the end, this is what counts. On his raised beach, higher up
still, MacDiarmid told us:

> We must reconcile ourselves to the stones,
> Not the stones to us.[34]

The stones transcend governments, principalities, powers. If our
work as teachers of literature is worth anything at all, it's because it
comes out of the stones. Look at Iraq, Rwanda, Darfur. Then look
at Loch Maree and its shining islands.

Underfunded as they are, Kim Stafford tells us 'education, language study, the arts, and cultural exchanges among the divided populations of the world are the highest priority of our time. These are the assets of peace.'[35]

That's the story that has to be told, over and over again, in the language we have, wherever we are, in defiance not only of the jargons of fashion and the vanities of parochialism but also even the orthodoxies of literary history. Gillespie lives. The written chronicles come from the lives, the people, the earth.

What is yielded then is a comprehensive vision of Scotland. A few writers might be understood and named as precedents: Scott, Gibbon and Gunn, MacDiarmid, from the 1920s (where he most of all established that the modern is the past reclaimed) to Morgan's *Sonnets from Scotland* in the 1980s, which he produced alongside Liz Lochhead's *Mary Queen of Scots Got Her Head Chopped Off* and Alasdair Gray's *Lanark* (1981) – all comprehensive works in their respective genres, poetry, play, novel, reasserting the complex distinctiveness of Scotland's multiple, singular, changing, essential identity.

And as we draw to a close, I'd like to remind ourselves of that identity now.

It's dark, probably misty outside, the sort of night I was in at the start of the lecture, with Wilson Harris speaking from the depths of his vulnerability.

Before we venture out, let's be reminded of the Scotland on our doorstep, and another trajectory from MacDiarmid to Morgan, supplied by Marshall Walker by way of New Zealand, from a journey made nearly a quarter of a century ago: old friends and living lands, real presences (see colour plates section):

We began with Wilson Harris speaking from the depths of his vulnerability. Let me give the last word to Edwin Morgan. I was talking to him yesterday evening, by phone, and he asked me to send his salutations and best wishes to all of us here today. Here he is as Pelagius, the author confronting his creators, who are only the people who will live after he has gone, remembering him as they will, creating, recreating his perennial message that only human grace is what we have, that we shouldn't be constrained by the lie of original sin, that what we make here is all we can hope to do, that what's on the margins, we should move to the centre – from the periphery, into the hub – take what's out of history and make history with it.

We can do it here as well as anywhere, can we not?

Counter-argument: yes we can.

But first I would like to thank the Dean of the Faculty of Arts, Elizabeth Moignard, who has been tremendous in her support of this day, and to thank Wendy Burt, Dr Nicky Trott, Pat Devlin, Professor Mike McMahon, Head of the School – some structures bring out the best in people, and the School structure does just that[36] – and all colleagues, staff, students, family – my sister Aileen, who flew over from Istanbul and has been looking after my parents today – friends who are here – my best teachers, Tim Cribb, who flew up from Cambridge this morning – and above all, my wife Rae.

Once upon a time in the west of Scotland . . .

> I, Morgan, whom the Romans call Pelagius
> Am back in my own place, my green Cathures
> By the frisky firth of salmon, by the open sea
> Not far, place of my name, at the end of things,
> As it must seem. But it is not a dream
> Those voyages, my hair grew white at the tiller,
> I have been where I say I have been,
> And my cheek still burns for the world.
>
>   *   *   *
>
> Sometimes when I stand on Blythswood Hill
> And strain my eyes (they are old now) to catch

Those changing lights of evening, and the clouds
Going their fiery way towards the firth,
I think we must just be ourselves at last
And wait like prophets – no, not wait, work! –
As prophets do, to see the props dissolve,
The crutches, threats, vain promises,
Altars, ordinances, comminations
Melt off into forgetfulness.
My robe flaps; a gull swoops; man is all.
Cathurian towers will ring this hill.
Engines unheard of yet will walk the Clyde.
I do not even need to raise my arms,
My blessing breathes with the earth.
It is for the unborn, to accomplish their will
With amazing, but only human, grace.[37]

Notes

1   Wilson Harris, 'The Fabric of the Imagination', in *The Radical Imagination: Lectures and Talks*, ed. Alan Riach and Mark Williams (Liège: L3 – Liège, Language and Literature / University of Liège, 1992), pp.69–79 (p.69).

2   Edwin Morgan, 'Introduction', in James Thomson, *The City of Dreadful Night* (1880; Edinburgh: Canongate Classics, 1993), pp.7–24 (pp.8–9).

3   Cited in Alan Bold, *MacDiarmid: Christopher Murray Grieve. A Critical Biography* (London: Paladin, 1990), p.204 and p.157, respectively.

4   John Berger, 'The Moment of Cubism', in *The White Bird: Writings*, ed. Lloyd Spencer (London: Chatto & Windus, 1985),

pp.159–88; *G.* (Harmondsworth: Penguin Books, 1972; 1976), p.149. I was quoting from memory. The actual sentence reads: 'Never again will a single story be told as though it were the only one.'

5   Hugh MacDiarmid, from 'Homage to Dunbar', in *Complete Poems*, Volume II, ed. Michael Grieve and W.R. Aitken (Manchester: Carcanet Press, 1994), pp.1265–66.

6   Donald Allen, ed., *The New American Poetry* (New York: Grove Press/London: Evergreen Books, 1960).

7   Hugh MacDiarmid, 'America's Example to Scottish Writers', *Jabberwock* (1959), quoted in its entirety in Alan Riach, 'Vitality So Abundant: MacDiarmid and the Americans', *Edinburgh Review*, no.97 (Spring 1997), pp.103–14.

8   Edwin Morgan, 'NIGERIA UNDATED REPORTED OCTOBER 1971', in *Collected Poems* (Manchester: Carcanet, 1996), p.219.

9   'The Informationists' was the term coined by Richard Price in the 1980s to identify a small number of poets including David Kinloch, Peter McCarey, Alan Riach and Price himself. The term drew attention to the idea that in a mass-media-saturated era, valuable information is at a premium, literally in terms of shelf-space in bookshops and libraries, or on the airwaves, in conversation, in what occupies language and time. Most of the poets in this group were also academics engaged in scholarly research and teaching, whose subsequent careers show various degrees of continued resistance to commercial priorities. My point here is that Morgan foreshadowed the concerns of these poets, and MacDiarmid before him, before the advent of mass media in fact. They both knew what was at stake.

10 Edwin Morgan, 'The don as poet or the poet as don', in *Nothing Not Giving Messages: reflections on work and life*, ed. Hamish Whyte (Edinburgh: Polygon, 1990), pp.194–95 (p.194).

11 'I tell you: one must have chaos in one, to give birth to a dancing star. I tell you: you still have chaos in you.' Friedrich Nietzsche, *Thus Spoke Zarathustra: A Book for Everyone and No One*, translated by R.J. Hollingdale (Harmondsworth: Penguin Books, 1972), p.46.

12 Hugh MacDiarmid, 'A New Movement in Scottish Literature', in *Selected Prose*, ed. Alan Riach (Manchester: Carcanet Press, 1992), pp.3–8 (p.3).

13 Bertolt Brecht, 'Zu den Lehrstücken – Theorie der Pedagogien', *Schriften* II, 129–30, quoted in Frederic Ewen, *Bertolt Brecht: His Life, His Art, and His Times* (London: Calder & Boyers, 1970), p.237.

14 Allen Curnow, 'Landfall in Unknown Seas', in *Early Days Yet: New and Collected Poems 1941–1997* (Manchester: Carcanet Press, 1997), pp.226–29 (p. 228).

15 T.S. Eliot, from *The Waste Land*, in *The Complete Poems and Plays* (London: Faber and Faber, 1977), pp.59–80 (p.73), line 384.

16 Ezra Pound, concluding sentence of 'Date Line' (*Make It New*, p.19): 'It is quite obvious that we do not all of us inhabit the same time.' Cited in Charles Olson & Robert Creeley, *The Complete Correspondence*, Volume 8, ed. George F. Butterick (Santa Rosa: Black Sparrow Press, 1987), p.261, note 49. In a letter to Olson dated 23 October 1951 (op. cit., pp.81–84), Creeley elaborates: 'Reading any definition of time, in the dictionary, gets you off to a somewhat abrupt recall – time came after sequence, etc. That "time" is a matter of something other than passage, that, like the image, it has its wanderings, actual – speed having exact relevance – in this way, almost plastic? Time certainly a variable,

in any case, odd as it wd sound, I suppose. But sequence, the hinge, since it gets back in, juxtaposition. That time occurs in terms of things, never abstract. Variation of time, even Ez' irony: we do not all of us inhabit the same time. We literally do not, all of us, inhabit the same time. There are speeds in it, deeper roots.' (p.83).

17   Allen Curnow, op. cit., p.228 and p.229.

18   Roderick Watson, *The Literature of Scotland* (Houndmills: Macmillan, 1984); Cairns Craig, General Editor, *The History of Scottish Literature*, 4 volumes (Aberdeen: Aberdeen University Press, 1987–88); Douglas Gifford and Dorothy McMillan, eds., *A History of Scottish Women's Writing* (Edinburgh: Edinburgh University Press, 1997); Duncan Macmillan, *Scottish Art 1460–1990* (Edinburgh: Mainstream, 1990); John Purser, *Scotland's Music: A History of the Traditional and Classical Music of Scotland from Early Times to the Present Day* (Edinburgh: Mainstream, 1992), Marshall Walker, *Scottish Literature Since 1707* (Harlow: Longman, 1996); Alan Riach, General Editor, *The Collected Works of Hugh MacDiarmid* (Manchester: Carcanet Press, initiated 1992).

19   Not quite in so many words. MacDiarmid calls Melville 'the greatest Socialist poet of Scots blood (albeit greater as a prose-writer than as a poet)' whose 'supreme glory is the authorship of *Moby-Dick*.' Hugh MacDiarmid, 'Signposts in Scottish Poetry Today', (1944–45), in *The Raucle Tongue: Hitherto uncollected prose*, Volume III, ed. Angus Calder, Glen Murray and Alan Riach (Manchester: Carcanet Press, 1998), pp.75–84 (p.83).

20   Jay Leyda, *The Melville Log: A Documentary Life of Herman Melville 1819–1891*, 2 volumes (New York: Gordian Press, 1969). See especially Volume Two, pp.526–27.

21 Alan Riach, 'Melville in Glasgow', in 'The View from the South Pacific', in Paul Henderson Scott, ed., *Spirits of the Age: Scottish Self Portraits* (Edinburgh: The Saltire Society, 2005), pp.325–37 (p.332).

22 Hugh MacDiarmid, 'Separatism', from *To Circumjack Cencrastus or The Curly Snake* (1930), in *Complete Poems*, Volume I, ed. Michael Grieve and W.R. Aitken (Manchester: Carcanet Press, 1993), pp.179–294 (p.273).

23 Ibid., p.289.

24 A.L. Brown and Michael Moss, *The University of Glasgow: 1451–2001* (Edinburgh: Edinburgh University Press, 2001), pp.96–97.

25 Henry S. Salt, Obituary of Herman Melville, *The Gentleman's Magazine* (1892), cited in Alan Riach, 'Demolition Man: An Introduction to *Contemporary Scottish Studies*', in Hugh MacDiarmid, *Contemporary Scottish Studies*, ed. Alan Riach (Manchester: Carcanet Press, 1995), pp.vii–xxxi (p.xxvi).

26 G. Gregory Smith, *Scottish Literature: Character and Influence* (London: Macmillan, 1919); see also Cairns Craig, 'The Study of Scottish Literature', in Ian Brown, General Editor; Thomas Owen Clancy, Murray Pittock, Period Editors; Susan Manning, co-editor, *The Edinburgh History of Scottish Literature, Volume One: From Columba to the Union (until 1707)*, (Edinburgh: Edinburgh University Press, 2007), pp.16–31.

27 Edwin Morgan, from 'A Demon', in *Cathures: New Poems 1997–2001* (Manchester: Carcanet Press, 2002), p.93.

28 William Johnstone, *Creative Art in Britain* (1950), cited in Alan Riach, 'William Johnstone', *Landfall: A New Zealand Quarterly*, no. 170 (June 1989), p.135.

29 Marshall Walker, 'On a Clear Day You Can See Lismore', unpublished keynote address at Scotland / New Zealand

Symposium, University of Glasgow (29–30 November, 2002), delivered 30 November.

30   Edwin Morgan, 'Lines for Wallace', in Lesley Duncan and Elspeth King, eds., *The Wallace Muse: Poems and artworks inspired by the life and legend of William Wallace* (Edinburgh: Luath Press, 2005), pp.15–16 (p.15).

31   Edwin Morgan, *A.D.: A Trilogy of Plays on the Life of Jesus* (Manchester; Carcanet Press, 2000), p.54.

32   Edwin Morgan, from 'The Fifth Gospel', in *Collected Poems* (Manchester; Carcanet Press, 1996), pp.259–60 (p.259).

33   Maurice Lindsay, *A Pocket Guide to Scottish Culture* (Glasgow: Maclellan, 1947); Sydney Goodsir Smith, *A Short Introduction to Scottish Literature* (Edinburgh: Serif Books, 1951); Douglas Gifford, Sarah Dunnigan and Alan MacGillivray, eds., *Scottish Literature in English and Scots* (Edinburgh: Edinburgh University Press, 2002); Ian Brown, General Editor, *The Edinburgh History of Scottish Literature*, 3 volumes (Edinburgh: Edinburgh University Press, 2007); Marco Fazzini, ed., *Alba Literaria: A History of Scottish Literature* (Venezia: Amos Edizioni, 2005); Roderick Watson, *The Literature of Scotland*, 2 volumes (Houndmills: Palgrave Macmillan, 2007).

34   Hugh MacDiarmid, 'On a Raised Beach', in *Complete Poems*, Volume I, ed. Michael Grieve and W.R. Aitken (Manchester: Carcanet Press, 1993), pp.422–33 (p.428), lines 219–20.

35   Kim Stafford, 'Afterword: Learning from Strangers', in *The Muses Among Us: Eloquent Listening and Other Pleasures of the Writer's Craft* (Athens and London: The University of Georgia Press, 2003), pp.122–33 (pp.131–32).

36   Glasgow University's School of English and Scottish Language and Literature (SESLL) is a single 'Unit of Assessment' in the

Research Assessment Exercise by which government evaluates scholarly research and rewards universities accordingly. The School is made up of three autonomous, financially self-determining Departments: the Department of English Language, the Department of English Literature and the Department of Scottish Literature. The School structure was established in 1996 and works to ensure respect for the different subjects within a context of mutual staff support and regular collaboration in teaching and research.

37 Edwin Morgan, from 'Pelagius', in *Cathures: New Poems 1997–2001* (Manchester: Carcanet Press, 2002), pp.9–11.

Afterword
Liz Lochhead

'Liberal and liberating developments in Scotland, Britain and beyond' are invoked by Douglas Gifford at the end of his foreword to this volume. To which we all say: yes please, more of these. These Inaugural Lectures – complementary but unique – themselves make a very significant liberal and liberating development. Their publication is an event in our culture, as was the occasion of their delivery.

Town and gown, just like the farmer and the ploughboy, should be friends. But some recent literary criticism, some recent 'theory' has been (to the outsider, the ordinary reader) very difficult to make head or tail of, very obscure indeed. It seems to make an exclusive little coterie out of the initiates of its jargon and to put out the message: you're too stupid, this is not for you. For me, one of the most refreshing things about my connection to Glasgow University as Writer in Residence and my temporary home in the Department of Scottish Literature has been to find a general distaste among the scholars I've encountered there for such an insular or self-serving, not to say onanistic, pursuit. The passion is for generous, illuminating criticism and research. For making connections, rejoicing in contradictions and in the humanity, the creativity, released by the largesse of spirit necessary to embrace both contradiction and connection. This passion has never been more clearly articulated than in these two brilliant lectures. (And I seek to use the word 'brilliant' as precisely as MacCaig – Alan Riach reminds us – would have. Meaning both 'displaying an adamantine intelligence that sends forth rays' and also, unashamedly, in the clichéd and quotidian vernacular, because they were – *are,* now they're in print – simply quite brilliant, and you can't say fairer than that.) There is a refusal here to make oppositional the 'creative' and the 'critical'. (Such would be a nonsense in a scholar like Alan Riach who is equally a poet, or in one like Nigel Leask who consistently quotes other poets on poets – Arnold on Burns, Moore on Byron.) If you've ever used the word 'academic' in a pejorative sense then reading this book now, or attending the lectures that day, will have thoroughly rid you of your prejudice.

One thing this book cannot do is replicate the theatricality, the immediacy, of the *performance* that day. The sense of occasion was palpable, utterly unstuffy, but with a genuine gravitas which only served to heighten the sparkle and dance of sheer delight in the interplay of ideas and intellects. This was important good fun. They spoke so well. The PowerPoint presentations *worked*. (In both senses of the word. Who could forget the flock of flying Scotsmen, kilted, displaying their bare arses to the world? Or the sublime evoked by the Ring of Brodgar, the Cuillins, the craggy faces of MacCaig, MacDiarmid, Mackay Brown, Crichton Smith, MacLean, Garioch – and our still gloriously here-with-us Morgan.) The new lecture theatre in the gloom of early December was lit up by jewels and shafts of generous, far-ranging, outward-reaching ideas and by the sheer skill, the practised lucidity, of Nigel Leask and Alan Riach who – as if it was easy – were able to impart, and to thoroughly engage us in our tussle with, such ideas.

Both professors used the chance to speak out passionately about the value, and the values, their discipline properly enshrines, asked very tough questions about exactly who, and what, it was all *for?* Were not afraid to question the prevailing market-forces-and-nothing-but-market-forces-led orthodoxies. Both were very rooted in, but certainly critical of, the real world. As you have read here, they dared to imagine, invoke, better worlds.

Yes, they spoke so well. If you want to know how to do such things with panache and make them memorable, then that was it. Oh, you should have been there. If you weren'y, you missed yourself, so you did. It was an education.

But whether you were or weren't there, now these lectures are in print the learning can go on. When the ideas come thick and fast as they did that day then we need to read, re-read, reconsider, hunt down with the help of the copious sources so meticulously credited the particular strands which we, personally, are just going to have to explore further now out of our newly awakened interest. I've already had to revisit (and with so much more pleasure than when I was at the school!) 'The Solitary Reaper' and then more and more of the Wordsworth I've so neglected since, and now I really need to know more about what Thomas Moore said about Byron's deep connection to Burns . . . Your imperative might be towards Cairns Craig's *Out of History,* evoked by Nigel Leask as '*quarrelling with the notion of Victorian Scotland as a cultural vacuum*'; or, prompted by Alan Riach, to, say, find out more about MacDiarmid's openness to all the post-colonial literatures he predicted (from '*Johannesberg or Sydney or Vancouver or Madras – or even Edinburgh*') in his wholehearted welcoming of Creeley, Ginsberg, Olson and other Americans to Scotland, just when you'd always thought him thoroughly antithetical to 'the beatnik in the Kailyerd' . . .

You will find the ripples from these lectures, so dense and yet so lightfooted in the dance, inexhaustible. MacDiarmid, in 'Gairmscoile', pleading the primacy of song, says '*It's soon', no sense that faddoms the herts o men*'. After reading, and re-reading, these lectures this woman ain't so sure. Or at least that it's an either/or. Nigel Leask quotes a wee phrase from Byron, in *Don Juan*, that I love: '*My heart flies to my head*'. The ideas we have in these lectures, so eruditely, yet so playfully, expressed, delight the heart as well as the mind, cross the shadow line between the two.

'*Find out what's on the periphery, move it to the centre. See how it changes the scene*' urges Alan Riach in his extended riff on MacDiarmid and Morgan. This is not a matter of mere canonicity or location, we can do such switcharound-and-sees with our minds and hearts also. Listen, really listen, to these lectures and we, or the world, will never be the same.

Copyright Acknowledgements